D1562243

Survey of American Poetry

Volume V
Civil War & Aftermath
1861-1889

Poetry Anthology Press

The World's Best Poetry

Survey of American Poetry

Survey of American Poetry

Volume V
Civil War & Aftermath
1861-1889

Prepared by
The Editorial Board, Granger Book Co., Inc.

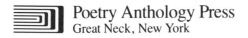

Poetry Anthology Press
Great Neck, New York

CONTENTS

Preface

The publications of **Poetry Anthology Press** constitute a comprehensive conspectus of international verse in English designed to form the core of a library's poetry collection. Covering the entire range of poetic literature, these anthologies encompass all topics and national literatures.

Each collection, published in a multivolume continuing series format, is devoted to a major area of the whole undertaking and contains complete author, title, and first line indexes. Biographical data is also provided.

The World's Best Poetry, with coverage through the 19th century, is topically classified and arranged by subject matter. Supplements keep the 10 volume foundation collection current and complete.

Survey of American Poetry is an anthology of American verse arranged chronologically in 10 volumes. Each volume presents a significant period of American poetic history, from 1607 to date.

INTRODUCTION

The years following the War between the States were a difficult period in American history. Paradoxically, while undergoing tremendous economic expansion, the young nation faced problems that threatened its very existence. Indeed, the industrialization of America was conducted on a scale unrivaled by developments in Europe. But in the aftermath of the Civil War, which had cost 600,000 lives and $8 billion, Americans were faced with the challange of healing wounds — both physical and psychological — and bringing back together the scattered ruins of a shattered nation. This was an overwhelming task. Blood resentments ranging on both sides of the Mason-Dixon line did little to aid in the process. Moreover, with the emancipation of the slaves, a large segment of the American population was left searching for a new role in society. For Walt Whitman, one of the most outspoken representatives of the period, this historical crossroads assumed global significance: it was of paramount importance to restore America — the great humanitarian experiment in democracy.

The Civil War, aside from its immediate concern with slavery, was essentially a struggle between agrarian and industrial — or "capitalistic" — democracy. When fighting broke out, America was an aggregate of farms, villages, and small towns; but, by the turn of the century, only about one third of the population still lived on rural territory. The triumph of the North, therefore, was primarily that of "industrialization" and "urbanization". Politics of the Reconstruction would seem to lend further credence to this notion. In effect, they were an attempt to force the South to conform to a northern ideal.

The South suffered dire destruction in the Civil War. Not only had it fallen to defeat, but it endured the more extensive damages in combat. For all practical purposes, the "scorched-earth" policy of Generals Sherman and Sheridan completely decimated the states of Georgia and Virginia; cities and farmhouses were burnt; seaports, railroads, and bridges were destroyed, and a campaign was launched in an effort to paralyze all forms of transportation. Furthermore, not only was Confederate property confiscated, but many individuals pursued dishonest appropriation of private assets. Confederate currency was declared worthless, banks closed down, and people lost entire fortunes. Finally, freedom was given to slaves who were largely unprepared, and a grave social problem arose as thousands began to move about, searching for food and trying to accustom themselves to an unfamiliar form of existance.

It is generally acknowledged that the presidental assassination in 1865 was a tragic blow to the development of the South, for it was Lincoln's intention to pursue a moderate course. Although it was the hope of the new president, Andrew Johnson, to follow a similar program, he was prevented from doing so by an extremely hostile Congress. Viewing the Confederate states as conquered provinces which had committed "state suicide" in seceding from the Union, northern politicians severely exacerbated the situation by adopting stern, punitive policies. Businessmen and government officials — derisively called "carpetbaggers" — descended upon the South and assumed positions of leadership. Using freedmen as political pawns, they excluded experienced local leaders and levied exorbitant taxes. Their administrations were riddled with graft, corruption, and the involvement of "scalawags" — southerners who collaborated with the carpetbaggers. In view of this, it has been suggested that the South suffered more during the Reconstruction than during the war itself.

Although the official process of reinstatement to the Union was difficult, by 1868 all of the Southern states except Mississippi, Texas, Virginia, and Georgia had been readmitted. Gradually, Northern sentiment towards the South relaxed; in 1872 Congress passed the Amnesty Act, restoring political rights, and four years later the defeat of the Republicans (who had spearheaded the Reconstruction) signalled the end of the difficult period. The establishment of new industries such as cotton milling, lumbering, and tobacco farming, was especially helpful in further promoting recovery.

In the process, it soon became evident that America was undergoing unparalleled growth. Pittsburg, Cleveland, and Detroit boomed as manufacturing centers. By 1860, Chicago had become the country's leading meat-packing center; between the middle and the end of the century its population grew tenfold to a total of 2 million inhabitants. Similarly, New York expanded from 500,000 to 3.5 million. At the same time, electricity was introduced on a nationwide scale, and the first transcontinental railroad was completed. In 1876, the telephone was invented. By the 1890s, the automobile had appeared. From 1850 to 1880, capital invested in manufacturing quadrupled, factory employment doubled, the national output of steel quintupled. Natural resources such as gold, silver, iron, coal, and oil were discovered in large amounts, and America become rich enough to subsidize its own economic development. Finally, fantastic fortunes were made by celebrated names such as Jay Gould, Jim Hill, Leland Stanford, Jim Fisk, Andrew Carnegie, J.P. Morgan and John D. Rockefeller.

Nevertheless, as we might expect, there were grave consequences. Namely, the unbridaled prosperity of a few developed at the expense of many. Accordingly, while the already poorly paid labor force was made to comply with increasingly unreasonable demands, government legislation did nothing to protect the interests of the common worker. "Darwinism" in turn began to play an important role, and scientific speculation concerning the "survival of the fittest" found an application in the environment of business and social interaction; it seemed to countenance selfishness and greed as a natural human predisposition. What is more, the moral framework provided by religion lost much of its authority, and there remained nothing other than what Thomas Carlyle aptly called a "cash nexus" between individuals. Nobody was his "brother's keeper", and there was no law but that of self-preservation. In order to obtain special favors, businessmen and politicians led an existence of ruthless cunning. They became self-styled captains of industry known as "robber barons" and accumulated vast shares of wealth by systematically squeezing out all competition. To take a well-known example, by 1882 John D. Rockefeller controlled over 90 per cent of the country's oil refineries.

The scandals of President Ulysses S. Grant's administration are indicative of the low moral climate of the time. Grant showed unabashed favoritism toward big business; he maintained high protective tarriffs and offered railroads all manner of federal subsidy. Indeed, there occurred during his first term the famous "Credit Mobilier Scandal" in which Congress was bribed to give financial support to the company. The "Whiskey Ring Fraud" saw distiller and treasury officials conspiring to defraud the government of revenue from the liquor tax. To make matters worse, Grant and his cabinet were known to have been intimately involved in improper dealings. and there was other questionable activity. For example, the "Black Friday Gold Conspiracy," was a plot executed by Jay Gould and Jim Fisk; it was conceived in order to corner the country's gold supply and to artificially inflate prices. In another instance, the Congress voted itself and the president a salary increase of 50 per cent — retroactive two years prior; this became known as the "Salary Grab Act." And it was in 1871 that the *New York Times* exposed William Marcy ("Boss") Tweed's plundering of the New York City treasury; through fake payments and graft he had managed to acquire from the city roughly $200 million.

In the initial stages, attempts to counteract such scandal and power play were sporadic. But, in 1877, strife between workers and employers mounted to a new level, and a nationally organized railroad strike paralyzed the entire country. Federal troops were called out, and scores of workers were killed and wounded. All of this, however, did not succeed in producing the necessary results, and workers were finally forced to accept a reduction in wages. Moreover, during the mid- to late seventies, a terrorist labor group known as the "Molly Maguires" committed a series of violent, murderous acts in the coal regions of Pennsylvania. Such events only exacerbated the situation; they promulgated a popular notion that labor organizations were dangerous, opposed to public interest, and should be curtailed.

Although the high-spirited optimism that animated American literature of the First Great Period (1830-1860) was not extinguished by the horrors of war or by the ensuing atmosphere of business and politics, it was inevitably tempered by new sobriety. As a nurse in an army hospital, Walt Whitman witnessed the destruction of war; nevertheless, he maintained an almost mystical faith in American democracy. In fact, the noted critic Roger Asselineau has observed that Whitman's vigorous populism was not concerned with the best means of securing an equal distribution of wealth, but rather with the American political system which he felt would allow for "the free development of individuals, and the full growth in all men of the moral and religious sense." Still, one notices a change in Whitman's post-Civil War verse: he somewhat curbs his nationalism and adopts the Hegelian view that evil is inevitable. That Whitman did not confuse ideals and flawed reality is evident in his prose work *Democratic Vistas* (1871); in this publication, he subjects his contemporaries to insightful, sometimes scathing criticism. However, it is Herman Melville who perhaps best illustrates many of the current dilemmas. His work documents an earnest search for faith; his poetry and prose chronicle the writer's thirst for a spiritual focus in an increasingly confusing and unstable world.

If Whitman is the poet of the macrocosm, Emily Dickinson can be viewed as the poet of the microcosm. Of course, this is something of an over-simplification. But, whereas Whitman is the poet of the open road, lustily celebrating the splendors of America from Atlantic to Pacific, Dickinson probes every depth of the private citizen's consciousness. Accordingly, she reacts to the same set of philosophical and metaphysical concerns that prompted the work of Whitman and Melville; but her approach is different and probably reflects her limited, circumscribed role as a woman in 19th-century American society. Poetry of this era also dealt with specific political issues: John Greenleaf Whittier championed the cause of the slaves; Henry Timrod and Paul Hamilton Hayne, on the other hand, spoke for the South. At the same time, Will Carleton and Sam Walter Foss espoused a populism that was sincere, somewhat romanticized, but not as profound as that of Whitman. And then there was the large body of poetry which remained steeped in early 19th-century English Romanticism. Although such verse does not attain the lofty heights of Whitman and Dickinson, it cannot be simply dismissed as backward or old-fashioned. On the contrary, it remains of interest to the serious student because of its wide acceptance at the time. Many lesser poets of the period were proud that their verse had little to do with the world they lived in; they viewed surrounding society as unworthy of poetic treatment. Thus, they held Whitman in disdain and regarded his choice of "common" subjects as vulgar and profane. Poets such as Edward Rowland Sill, Silas Weir Mitchell, and Elizabeth Akers are associated primarily with the kind of verse that mainstream America *wanted* to read; they reflect the somewhat simple, nostalgic, and naive attitudes of an era rapidly vanishing from the nation's consciousness.

EXPLANATORY NOTES

The present anthology is arranged chronologically. Its aim is (a) to provide the reader with a sense of the development of verse during the historical period and (b) to help place select works within the span of each poet's creative output. Accordingly, it lists the poets in sequence— by date of birth—and, wherever possible, gives the date of individual poems.

Words are spelled as they appear in the original sources; punctuation, capitalization, and usage are treated the same way. No attempt has been made to reconcile resulting inconsistencies. This, however, should not hinder a basic appreciation of the material. In some cases, the poems entered constitute selections; these are chosen to convey to the reader the essence of a major work which is too long to publish in the context of the anthology.

Authors, titles, and first lines are arranged in a single alphabetical listing in the Index. Poet names are in boldface; poem titles are in italics; and poem first lines are enclosed in quotation marks. When a title and first line are identical, only the title is given.

JOHN GREENLEAF WHITTIER [1807-1892]

John Greenleaf Whittier was born into a relatively poor line of Quakers from Haverhill, Massachusetts. As a teenager working on the family farm, however, he showed an unusual gift for poetry. In view of this, his sister Mary secretly sent one of his poems "The Exile's Departure" to the *Free Press,* a publication edited by the famous abolitionist William Lloyd Garrison. This proved to be a turning point in the young man's life. Garrison was so impressed that he published the poem and, at the same time, invited Whittier to obtain an education at Haverhill Academy. Whittier's close contact with Garrison's powerful personality during these years had a lasting impact; it triggered his involvement with radical ideas and especially the cause of abolitionism.

Upon finishing school in 1828, Whittier went to Boston where he worked as editor and writer for the important political journal *The American Manufacturer.* Two years later, he moved to Hartford to work with *The New England Weekly Review.* In 1833, he published a pamphlet entitled *Justice and Expediency* which helped promote the cause of the reknowned American Anti-Slavery Society. During this period, he also wrote a great deal of poetry expressing abolitionist sentiments.

In 1837, Whittier went to Philadelphia where he edited *The Pennsylvania Freeman.* Failing health, however, soon curtailed his activities so that in 1840 he was forced to return to Massachusetts. For the remaining years, until his death in 1892, he led a peaceful life in Amesbury with his sister. During this time he wrote many of his better known works.

Ichabod

So fallen! so lost! the light withdrawn
    Which once he wore!
The glory from his gray hairs gone
    Forevermore!

Revile him not, the Tempter hath
    A snare for all;
And pitying tears, not scorn and wrath,
    Befit his fall!

Oh, dumb be passion's stormy rage,
    When he who might
Have lighted up and led his age,
    Falls back in night.

Scorn! would the angels laugh, to mark
    A bright soul driven,
Fiend-goaded, down the endless dark,
    From hope and heaven!

Let not the land once proud of him
    Insult him now,
Nor brand with deeper shame his dim,
    Dishonored brow.

But let its humbled sons, instead,
    From sea to lake,

A long lament, as for the dead,
    In sadness make.

Of all we loved and honored, naught
        Save power remains;
A fallen angel's pride of thought,
        Still strong in chains.

All else is gone; from those great eyes
        The soul has fled:
When faith is lost, when honor dies,
        The man is dead!

Then pay the reverence of old days
        To his dead fame;
Walk backward, with averted gaze,
        And hide the shame!

Skipper Ireson's Ride [1860]

Of all the rides since the birth of time,
Told in story or sung in rhyme,—
On Apuleius's Golden Ass,
Or one-eyed Calender's horse of brass,
Witch astride of a human back,
Islam's prophet on Al-Borák,—
The strangest ride that ever was sped
Was Ireson's, out from Marblehead!
    Old Floyd Ireson, for his hard heart,
    Tarred and feathered and carried in a cart
    By the women of Marblehead!

Body of turkey, head of owl,
Wings a-droop like a rained-on fowl,
Feathered and ruffled in every part,
Skipper Ireson stood in the cart.
Scores of women, old and young.
Strong of muscle, and glib of tongue,
Pushed and pulled up the rocky lane,
Shouting and singing the shrill refrain:
    "Here's Flud Oirson, fur his horrd horrt,
    Torr'd an' futherr'd an' corr'd in a corrt
    By the women o' Morble'ead!

Wrinkled scolds with hands on hips.
Girls in bloom of cheek and lips,
Wild-eyed, free-limbed, such as chase
Bacchus round some antique vase,
Brief of skirts, with ankles bare,
Loose of kerchief and loose of hair,
With conch-shells blowing and fish-horns' twang,
    "Here's Flud Oirson, fur his horrd horrt,
    Torr'd an' futherr'd an' corr'd in a corrt
    By the women o' Morble'ead!

Small pity for him!—He sailed away
From a leaking ship in Chaleur Bay,—
Sailed away from a sinking wreck,
With his own town's-people on her deck!
"Lay by! lay by!" they called to him.
Back he answered, "Sink or swim!
Brag of your catch of fish again!"
And off he sailed through the fog and rain!
   Old Floyd Ireson, for his hard heart,
   Tarred and feathered and carried in a cart
    By the women of Marblehead!

Fathoms deep in dark Chaleur
That wreck shall lie forevermore.
Mother and sister, wife and maid,
Looked from the rocks of Marblehead
Over the moaning and rainy sea,—
Looked for the coming that might not be!
What did the winds and the sea-birds say
Of the cruel captain who sailed away?—
   Old Floyd Ireson, for his hard heart,
   Tarred and feathered and carried in a cart
    By the women of Marblehead!

Through the street, on either side,
Up flew windows, doors swung wide;
Sharp-tongued spinsters, old wives gray,
Treble lent the fish-horn's bray.
Sea-worn grandsires, cripple-bound,
Hulks of old sailors run aground,
Shook head, and fist, and hat, and cane,
And cracked with curses the hoarse refrain:
   "Here's Flud Oirson, fur his horrd horrt,
   Torr'd an' futherr'd an' corr'd in a corrt
    By the women o' Morble'ead!

Sweetly along the Salem road
Bloom of orchard and lilac showed.

Little the wicked skipper knew
Of the fields so green and the sky so blue.
Riding there in his sorry trim,
Like an Indian idol glum and grim,
Scarcely he seemed the sound to hear
Of voices shouting, far and near:
   "Here's Flud Oirson, fur his horrd horrt,
   Torr'd an' futherr'd an' corr'd in a corrt
     By the women o' Morble'ead!"

"Hear me, neighbors!" at last he cried,—
"What to me is this noisy ride?
What is the shame that clothes the skin
To the nameless horror that lives within?
Walking or sleeping, I see a wreck,
And hear a cry from a reeling deck!
Hate me and curse me,—I only dread
The hand of God and the face of the dead!"
   Said old Floyd Ireson, for his hard heart,
   Tarred and feathered and carried in a cart
     By the women of Marblehead!

Then the wife of the skipper lost at sea
Said, "God has touched him! why should we!"
Said an old wife mourning her only son,
"Cut the rogue's tether and let him run!"
So with soft relentings and rude excuse,
Half scorn, half pity, they cut him loose,
And gave him a cloak to hide him in,
And left him alone with his shame and sin.
   Poor Floyd Ireson, for his hard heart,
   Tarred and feathered and carried in a cart
     By the women of Marblehead!

Abraham Davenport

In the old days (a custom laid aside
With breeches and cocked hats) the people sent
Their wisest men to make the public laws.
And so, from a brown homestead, where the Sound
Drinks the small tribute of the Mianas,
Waved over by the woods of Rippowams,

And hallowed by pure lives and tranquil deaths,
Stamford sent up to the councils of the State
Wisdom and grace in Abraham Davenport.

'Twas on a May-day of the far old year
Seventeen hundred eighty, that there fell
Over the bloom and sweet life of the Spring,
Over the fresh earth and the heaven of noon,
A horror of great darkness, like the night
In day of which the Norland sagas tell,—
The Twilight of the Gods. The low-hung sky
Was black with ominous clouds, save where its rim
Was fringed with a dull glow, like that which climbs
The crater's side from the red hell below.
Birds ceased to sing, and all the barn-yard fowls
Roosted; the cattle at the pasture bars
Lowed, and looked homeward; bats on leathern wings
Flitted abroad; the sounds of labor died;
Men prayed, and women wept; all ears grew sharp
To hear the doom-blast of the trumpet shatter
The black sky, that the dreadful face of Christ
Might look from the rent clouds, not as He looked
A loving guest at Bethany, but stern
As Justice and inexorable Law.

Meanwhile in the old State House, dim as ghosts,
Sat the lawgivers of Connecticut,
Trembling beneath their legislative robes.
"It is the Lord's Great Day! Let us adjourn,"

Some said; and then, as if with one accord,
All eyes were turned to Abraham Davenport.
He rose, slow cleaving with his steady voice
The intolerable hush. "This well may be
The Day of Judgement which the world awaits;
But be it so or not, I only know
My present duty, and my Lord's command
To occupy till He come. So at the post
Where He hath set me in His providence,
I choose, for one, to meet Him face to face,—
No faithless servant frightened from my task,
But ready when the Lord of the harvest calls;
And therefore, with all reverence, I would say,
Let God do His work, we will see to ours.
Bring in the candles." And they brought them in.

    Then by the flaring lights the Speaker read,
Albeit with husky voice and shaking hands,
An act to amend an act to regulate
The shad and alewive fisheries. Whereupon
Wisely and well spake Abraham Davenport,
Straight to the question, with no figures of speech
Save the ten Arab signs, yet not without
The shrewd dry humor natural to the man:
His awe-struck colleagues listening all the while,
Between the pauses of his argument,
To hear the thunder of the wrath of God
Break from the hollow trumpet of the cloud.

    And there he stands in memory to this day,
Erect, self-poised, a rugged face, half seen
Against the background of unnatural dark,
A witness to the ages as they pass,
That simple duty hath no place for fear.

Song of Slaves in the Desert

Where are we going? where are we going,
Where are we going, Rubee?
Lord of peoples, lord of lands,
Look across these shining sands,

Through the furnace of the noon,
Through the white light of the moon.
Strong the Ghiblee wind is blowing,
Strange and large the world is growing!
Speak and tell us where we are going,
        Where are we going, Rubee?

Bornou land was rich and good,
Wells of water, fields of food,
Dourra fields, and bloom of bean,
And the palm-tree cool and green:
Bornou land we see no longer,
Here we thirst and here we hunger,
Here the Moor-man smites in anger:
        Where are we going, Rubee?

When we went from Bornou land,
We were like the leaves and sand,
We were many, we are few;
Life has one, and death has two:
Whitened bones our path are showing,
Thou All-seeing, thou All knowing!
Hear us, tell us, where are we going,
        Where are we going, Rubee?

Moons of marches from our eyes
Bornou land behind us lies;
Stranger round us day by day
Bends the desert circle gray;
Wild the waves of sand are flowing,
Hot the winds above them blowing,—

Lord of all things! where are we going?
   Where are we going, Rubee?

We are weak, but Thou are strong;
Short our lives, but Thine is long;
We are blind, but Thou hast eyes;
We are fools, but Thou art wise!
Thou, our morrow's pathway knowing
Through the strange world round us growing,
Hear us, tell us where are we going,
   Where are we going, Rubee?

Divine Compassion [1869]

Long since, a dream of heaven I had,
   And still the vision haunts me oft;
I see the saints in white robes clad,
   The martyrs with their palms aloft;
But hearing still, in middle song,
   The ceaseless dissonance of wrong;
And shrinking, with hid faces, from the strain
Of sad, beseeching eyes, full of remorse and pain.

The glad song falters to a wail,
   The harping sinks to low lament;
Before the still unlifted veil
   I see the crowned foreheads bent,
Making more sweet the heavenly air
   With breathings of unselfish prayer;
And a Voice saith: "O Pity which is pain,
O Love that weeps, fill up my sufferings which remain!

"Shall souls redeemed by me refuse
   To share my sorrow in their turn?
Or, sin-forgiven, my gift abuse
   Of peace with selfish unconcern?

Has saintly ease no pitying care?
Has faith no work, and love no prayer?
While sin remains, and souls in darkness dwell,
Can heaven itself be heaven, and look unmoved on hell?"

Then through the Gates of Pain, I dream,
    A wind of heaven blows coolly in;
Fainter the awful discords seem,
    The smoke of torment grows more thin,
Tears quench the burning soil, and thence
    Spring sweet, pale flowers of penitence
And through the dreary realm of man's despair,
Star-crowned an angel walks, and lo! God's hope is there!

Is it a dream? Is heaven so high
    That pity cannot breathe its air?
Its happy eyes forever dry,
    It's holy lips without a prayer!
My God! my God! if thither led
    By Thy free grace unmerited,
No crown nor palm be mine, but let me keep
A heart that still can feel, and eyes that still can weep.

My Playmate [1860]

The pines were dark on Ramoth hill,
    Their song was soft and low;
The blossoms in the sweet May wind
    Were falling like the snow.

The blossoms drifted at our feet,
    The orchard birds sang clear;
The sweetest and the saddest day
    It seemed of all the year.

For, more to me than birds or flowers,
    My playmate left her home,
And took with her the laughing spring,
    The music and the bloom.

She kissed the lips of kith and kin,
    She laid her hand in mine:
What more could ask the bashful boy
    Who fed her father's kine?

She left us in the bloom of May:
    The constant years told o'er
Their seasons with as sweet May morns,
    But she came back no more.

I walk, with noiseless feet, the round
    Of uneventful years;
Still o'er and o'er I sow the spring
    And reap the autumn ears.

She lives where all the golden year
    Her summer roses blow;
The dusky children of the sun
    Before her come and go.

There haply with her jewelled hands
    She smooths her silken gown,—

No more the homespun lab wherein
  I shook the walnuts down.

The wild grapes wait us by the brook,
  The brown nuts on the hill,
And still the May-day flowers make sweet
  The woods of Follymill.

The lilies blossom in the pond,
  The bird builds in the tree,
The dark pines sing on Ramoth hill
  The slow song of the sea.

I wonder if she thinks of them,
  And how the old time seems,—
If ever the pines of Ramoth wood
  Are sounding in her dreams.

I see her face, I hear her voice;
  Does she remember mine?
And what to her is now the boy
  Who fed her father's kine?

What cares she that the orioles build
  For other eyes than ours,—
That other hands with nuts are filled,
  And other laps with flowers?

O playmate in the golden time!
  Our mossy seat is green,
Its fringing violets blossom yet,
  The old trees o'er it lean.

The winds so sweet with birch and fern
  A sweeter memory blow;
And there in spring the veeries sing
  The song of long ago.

And still the pines of Ramoth wood
Are moaning like the sea,—
The moaning of the sea of change
Between myself and thee!

Snow-Bound [1866]

A Winter Idyl

To the Memory of the Household It Describes
This Poem Is Dedicated by the Author

The sun that brief December day
Rose cheerless over the hills of gray,
And, darkly circled, gave at noon
A sadder light than waning moon.
Slow tracing down the thickening sky
Its mute and ominous prophecy,
A portent seeming less than threat,
It sank from sight before it set.
A chill no coat, however stout,
Of homespun stuff could quite shut out,
A hard, dull bitterness of cold,
That checked, mid-vein, the circling race
Of life-blood in the sharpened face,
The coming of the snow-storm told.
The wind blew east; we heard the roar
Of Ocean on his wintry shore,
And felt the strong pulse throbbing there
Beat with low rhythm our inland air.

Meanwhile we did our nightly chores,—
Brought in the wood from out of doors,
Littered the stalls, and from the mows
Raked down the herd's-grass for the cows:
Heard the horse whinnying for his corn;
And, sharply clashing horn on horn,

Impatient down the stanchion rows
The cattle shake their walnut bows;
While, peering from his early perch
Upon the scaffold's pole of birch,
The cock his crested helmet bent
And down his querulous challenge sent.

Unwarmed by any sunset light
The gray day darkened into night,
A night made hoary with the swarm
And whirl-dance of the blinding storm,
As zigzag, wavering to and fro,
Crossed and recrossed the wingèd snow:
And ere the early bedtime came
The white drift piled the window-frame,
And through the glass the clothes-line posts
Looked in like tall and sheeted ghosts.

So all night long the storm roared on:
The morning broke out without a sun;
In tiny spherule traced with lines,
Of Nature's geometric signs,
In starry flake, and pellicle,
All day the hoary meteor fell;
And, when the second morning shone,
We looked upon a world unknown,
On nothing we could call our own.
Around the glistening wonder bent
The blue walls of the firmament,
No clouds above, no earth below,—
A universe of sky and snow!

The old familiar sights of ours
Took marvellous shapes; strange domes and towers
Rose up where sty or corn-crib stood,
Or garden-wall, or belt of wood;
A smooth white mound the brush-pile showed,
A fenceless drift what once was road;
The bridle-post an old man sat

With loose-flung coat and high cocked hat;
The well-curb had a Chinese roof;
And even the long sweep, high aloof,
In its slant splendor, seemed to tell
Of Pisa's leaning miracle.

A prompt, decisive man, no breath
Our father wasted: "Boys, a path!"
Well pleased, (for when did farmer boy
Count such a summons less than joy?)
Our buskins on our feet we drew;
With mittened hands, and caps drawn low,
To guard our necks and ears from snow,
We cut the whiteness through.
And, where the drift was deepest, made
A tunnel walled and overlaid
With dazzling crystal: we had read
Of rare Aladdin's wonderous cave,
And to our own his name we gave,
With many a wish the luck were ours
To test his lamp's supernal powers.
We reached the barn with merry din,
And roused the prisoned brutes within.
The old horse thrust his long head out,
And grave with wonder gazed about;
The cock his lusty greeting said,
And forth his speckled harem led;
The oxen lashed their tales, and hooked,
And mild reproach of hunger looked;
The hornëd patriarch of the sheep,
Like Egypt's Amun roused from sleep,
Shook his sage head with gesture mute,
And emphasized with stamp of foot

All day the gusty north-wind bore
The loosening drift is breath before;
Low circling round its southern zone,
The sun through dazzling snow-mist shone.
No church-bell lent its Christian tone

To the savage air, no social smoke
Curled over woods of snow-hung oak.
A solitude made more intense
By dreary-voicëd elements,
The shrieking of the mindless wind,
The moaning tree-boughs swaying blind,
And on the glass the unmeaning beat
Of ghostly finger-tips of sleet.
Beyond the circle of our hearth
No welcome sound of toil or mirth
Unbound the spell, and testified
Of human life and thought outside.
We minded that the sharpest ear
The buried brooklet could not hear,
The music of whose liquid lip
Had been to us companionship,
And, in our lonely life, had grown
To have an almost human tone.

As night drew on, and, from the crest
Of wooded knolls that ridged the west,
The sun, a snow-blown traveller, sank
From sight beneath the smothering bank,
We piled, with care, our nightly stack
Of wood against the chimney-back,—
The oaken log, green, huge, and thick,
And on its top the stout back-stick;
The knotty forestick laid apart,
And filled between with curious art
The ragged brush; then hovering near,
We watched the first red blaze appear,
Heard the sharp crackle, caught the gleam
On whitewashed wall and sagging beam,
Until the old, rude-furnished room
Burst, flower-like, into rosy bloom;
While radiant with a mimic flame
Outside the sparkling drift became,
And through the bare-boughed lilac-tree
Our own warm hearth seemed blazing free.

The crane and pendent trammels showed,
The Turks' heads on the andirons glowed;
While childish fancy, prompt to tell
The meaning of the miracle,
Whispered the old rhyme: *"Under the tree,*
When fire outdoors burns merrily,
There the witches are making tea."

The moon above the eastern wood
Shone at its full; the hill-range stood
Transfigured in the silver flood,
Its blown snows flashing cold and keen,
Dead white, save where some sharp ravine
Took shadow, or the sombre green
Of hemlocks turned to pitchy black
Against the whiteness at their back
For such a world and such a night
Most fitting that unwarming light,
Which only seemed where'er it fell
To make the coldness visible.

Shut in from all the world without,
We sat the clean-winged hearth about,
Content to let the north-wind roar
In baffled rage at pane and door,
While the red logs before us beat
The frost-line back with tropic heat;
And ever, when a louder blast
Shook beam and rafter as it passed,
The merrier up its roaring draught
The great throat of the chimney laughed;
The house-dog on his paws outspread
Laid to the fire his drowsy head,
The cat's dark silhouette on the wall
A couchant tiger's seemed to fall;
And, for the winter fireside meet,
Between the andirons' straddling feet,
The mug of cider simmered slow,

The apples sputtered in a row,
And, close at hand, the basket stood
With nuts from brown October's wood.

What matter how the night behaved?
What matter how the north-wind raved?
Blow high, blow low, not all its snow
Could quench our hearth-fire's ruddy glow.
O Time and Change!—with hair as gray
As was my sire's that winter day,
How strange it seems, with so much gone
Of live and love, to still live on!
Ah, brother! only I and thou
Are left of all that circle now,—
The dear home faces whereupon
That fitfull firelight paled and shone.
Henceforward, listen as we will,
The voices of that hearth are still;
Look where we may, the wide earth o'er,
Those lighted faces smile no more.
We tread the paths their feet have worn,
    We sit beneath their orchard trees,
    We hear, like them, the hum of bees
And rustle of the bladed corn;
We turn the pages that they read,
    Their written words we linger o'er,
But in the sun they cast no shade,
No voice is heard, no sign is made,
    No step is on the conscious floor!
Yet Love will dream, and Faith will trust,
(Since He who knows our need is just,)
That somehow, somewhere, meet we must.
Alas for him who never sees
The stars shine through his cypress-trees!
Who, hopeless, lays his dead away,
Nor looks to see the breaking day
Across the mournful marbles play!
Who hath not learned, in hours of faith,
    The truth to flesh and sense unknown,

That Life is ever lord of Death,
And Love can never lose its own!

We sped the time with stories old,
Wrought puzzles out, and riddles told,
Or stammered from our school-book lore
"The Chief of Gambia's golden shore."
How often since, when all the land
Was clay in Slavery's shaping hand,
As if a far-blown trumpet stirred
The languorous sin-sick air, I heard:
"Does not the voice of reason cry,
    Claim the first right which Nature gave,
From the red scourge of bondage fly,
    Nor deign to live a burdened slave!"
Our father rode again his ride
On Memphremagog's wooded side;
Sat down again to moose and samp
In trapper's hut and Indian camp;
Lived o'er the old idyllic ease
Beneath St. François' hemlock-trees;
Again for him the moonlight shone
On Norman cap and bodiced zone;
Again he heard the violin play
Which led the village dance away,
And mingled in its merry whirl
The grandam and the laughing girl.
Or, nearer home, our steps he led
Where Salisbury's level marshes spread
    Mile-wide as flies the laden bee;
Where merry mowers, hale and strong,
Swept, scythe on scythe, their swaths along
    The low green prairies of the sea.
We shared the fishing off Boar's Head,
    And round the rocky Isles of Shoals
    The hake-broil on the drift-wood coals;
The chowder on the sand-beach made,
Dipped by the hungry, steaming hot,
With spoons of clam-shell from the pot.

We heard the tales of witchcraft old,
And dream and sign and marvel told
To sleepy listeners as they lay
ʹStretched idly on the salted hay,
Adrift along the winding shores,
When favoring breezes deigned to blow
The square sail of the gundelow
And idle lay the useless oars.

Our mother, while she turned her wheel
Or run the new-knit stocking-heel,
Told how the Indian hordes came down
At midnight on Cocheco town,
And how her own great-uncle bore
His cruel scalp-mark to fourscore.
Recalling, in her fitting phrase,
    So rich and picturesque and free,
    (The common unrthymed poetry
Of simple life and country ways,)
The story of her early days,—
She made us welcome to her home;
Old hearths grew wide to give us room;
We stole with her a frightened look
At the gray wizard's conjuring-book,
The fame whereof went far and wide
Through all the simple country side;
We heard the hawks at twilight play,
The boat-horn on Piscataqua,
The loon's weird laughter far away;
We fished her little trout-brook, knew
What flowers in wood and meadow grew,
What sunny hillsides autumn-brown
She climbed to shake the ripe nuts down,
Saw where in sheltered cove and bay
The ducks' black squadron anchored lay,
And heard the wild-geese calling loud
Beneath the gray November cloud.

Then, haply, with a look more grave,

And soberer tone, some tale she gave
From painful Sewel's ancient tome,
Beloved in every Quaker home,
Of faith fire-winged by martyrdom,
Or Chalkley's Journal, old and quaint,—
Gentlest of skippers, rare sea saint!—
Who, when the dreary calms prevailed,
And water-butt and bread cask failed,
And cruel, hungry eyes pursued
His portly presence mad for food,
With dark hints muttered under breath
Of casting lots for life or death,
Offered, if Heaven withheld supplies,
To be himself the sacrifice.
Then, suddenly, as if to save
The good man from his living grave,
A ripple on the water grew,
A school of porpoise flashed in view.
"Take, eat," he said, "and be content;
These fishes in my stead are sent
By Him who gave the tangled ram
To spare the child of Abraham."

Our uncle, innocent of books,
Was rich in lore of fields and brooks,
The ancient teachers never dumb
Of Nature's unhoused lyceum.
In moons and tides and weather wise,
He read the clouds as prophecies,
And foul or fair could well divine,
By many an occult hint and sign,
Holding the cunning-warded keys
To all the woodcraft mysteries;
Himself to Nature's heart so near
That all her voices in his ear
Of beast or bird had meanings clear,
Like Apollonius of old,
Who knew the tales the sparrows told,
Or Hermes, who interpreted

What the sag cranes of Nilus said;
A simple, guileless, childlike man,

Content to live where life began;
Strong only on his native grounds,
The little world of sights and sounds
Whose girdle was the parish bounds,
Whereof his fondly partial pride
The common features magnified,
As Surrey hills to mountains grew
In White of Selborne's loving view,—
He told how teal and loon he shot,
And how the eagle's eggs he got,
The feats on pond and river done,
The prodigies of rod and gun;
Till, warming with the tales he told,
Forgotten was the outside cold,
The bitter wind unheeded blew,
From ripening corn the pigeons flew,
The partridge drummed i' the wood, the mink
Went fishing down the river-brink.
In fields with bean or clover gay,
The woodchuck, like a hermit gray,
    Peered from the doorway of his cell;
The muskrat plied the mason's trade,
And tier by tier his mud-walls laid;
And from the shagbark overhead
    The grizzled squirrel dropped his shell.

Next, the dear aunt, whose smile of cheer
And voice in dreams I see and hear,—
The sweetest woman ever Fate
Perverse denied a household mate,
Who, lonely, homeless, not the less
Found peace in love's unselfishness,
And welcome whereso'er she went,
A calm and gracious element,
Whose presence seemed the sweet income
And womanly atmosphere of home,—

Called up her girlhood memories,
The huskings and the apple-bees,
The sleigh-rides and the summer sails,
Weaving through all the poor details

And homespun warp of circumstance
A golden woof-thread of romance.
For well she kept her genial mood
And simple faith of maidenhood;
Before her still a cloud-land lay,
The mirage loomed across her way;
The morning dew, that dries so soon
With others, glistened at her noon;
Through years of toil and soil and care,
From glossy trees to thin gray hair,
All unprofaned she held apart
The virgin fancies of the heart.
Be shame to him of woman born
Who hath for such but thought of scorn.

There, too, our elder sister plied
Her evening task the stand beside;
A full, rich nature, free to trust,
Truthful and almost sternly just,
Impulsive, earnest, prompt to act,
And make her generous thought a fact,
Keeping with many a light disguise
The secret of self-sacrifice.
O heart sore-tried! thou hast the best
That Heaven itself could give thee, —rest,
Rest from all bitter thoughts and things!
    How many a poor one's blessing went
    With thee beneath the low green tent
Whose curtain never outward swings!

As one who held herself a part
Of all she saw, and let her heart
    Against the household bosom lean,

Upon the motley-braided mat
Our youngest and our dearest sat,
Lifting her large, sweet, asking eyes,
    Now bathed in the unfading green
And holy peace of Paradise.
Oh, looking from some heavenly hill,

    Or from the shade of saintly palms,
    Or silver reach of river calms,
Do those large eyes behold me still?
With me one little year ago:—
The chill weight of the winter snow
    For months upon her grave has lain;
And now, when summer south-winds blow
    And brier and harebell bloom again,
I tread the pleasant paths we trod,
I see the violet-sprinkled sod
Whereon she leaned, too frail and weak
The hillside flowers she loved to seek,
Yet following me where'er I went
With dark eyes full of love's content.
The birds are glad; the brier-rose fills
The air with sweetness; all the hills
Stretch green to June's unclouded sky;
But still I wait with ear and eye
For something gone which should be nigh,
A loss in all familiar things,
In flower that blooms, and bird that sings.
And yet, dear heart! remembering thee,
    Am I not richer than of old?
Safe in thy immorality,
    What change can reach the wealth I hold?
    What chance can mar the pearl and gold
Thy love hath left in trust with me?
And while in life's late afternoon,
    Where cool and long the shadows grow,
I walk to meet the night that soon
    Shall shape and shadow overflow,
I cannot feel that thou art far,

Since near at need the angels are;
And when the sunset gates unbar,
   Shall I not see thee waiting stand,
And, white against the evening star,
   The welcome of thy beckoning hand?

Brisk wielder of the birch and rule,
The master of the district school

Held at the fire his favored place,
Its warm glow lit a laughing face
Fresh-hued and fair, where scarce appeared
The uncertain prophecy of beard.
He teased the mitten-blinded cat,
Played cross-pins on my uncle's hat,
Sang songs, and told us what befalls
In classic Dartmouth's college halls.
Born the wild Northern hills among,
From whence his yeoman father wrung
By patient toil subsistence scant,
Not competence and yet not want,
He early gained the power to pay
His cheerful, self-reliant way;
Could doff at ease his scholar's gown
To peddle wares from town to town;
Or through the long vacation's reach
In lonely lowlands districts teach,
Where all the droll experience found
At stranger hearths in boarding round,
The moonlit skater's keen delight,
The sleigh-drive through the frosty night,
The rustic party, with its rough
Accompaniment of blind-man's-buff,
And whirling-plate, and forfeits paid,
His winter task a pastime made.
Happy the snow-locked homes wherein
He tuned his merry violin,
Or played the athlete in the barn,
Or held the good dame's winding-yarn,

Or mirth-provoking versions told
Of classic legends rare and old,
Wherein the scenes of Greece and Rome
Had all the commonplace of home,
And little seemed at best the odds
'Twixt Yankee pedlers and old gods;
Where Pindus-born Arachthus took
The guise of any grist-mill brook,
And dread Olympus at his will
Became a huckleberry hill.

A careless boy that night he seemed;
    But at his desk he had the look
And air of one who wisely schemed,
    And hostage from the future took
    In trainëd thought and lore of book.
Large-brained, clear-eyed, of such as he
Shall Freedom's young apostles be,
Who, following in War's bloody trail,
Shall every lingering wrong assail;
All chains from limb and spirit strike,
Uplift the black and white alike;
Scatter before their swift advance
The darkness and the ignorance,
The pride, the lust, the squalid sloth,
Which nurtured Treason's monstrous growth,
Made murder pastime, and the hell
Of prison-torture possible;
The cruel lie of caste refute,
Old forms remould, and substitute
For Slavery's lash the freeman's will,
For blind routine, wise-handed skill;
A school-house plant on every hill,
Stretching in radiate nerve-lines thence
The quick wires of intelligence;
Till North and South together brought
Shall own the same electric thought,
In peace a common flag salute,
And, side by side in labor's free

And unresentful rivalry,
Harvest the fields wherein they fought.

Another guest that winter night
Flashed back from lustrous eyes the light.
Unmarked by time, and yet not young,
The honeyed music of her tongue
And words of meekness scarcely told
A nature passionate and bold,
Strong, self-concentred, spurning guide,
Its milder features dwarfed beside
Her unbent will's majestic pride.

She sat among us, at the best,
A not unfeared, half-welcomed guest,
Rebuking with her cultured phrase
Our homeliness of words and ways.
A certain pard-like, treacherous grace
Swayed the lithe limbs and drooped the lash,
Lent the white teeth their dazzling flash;
And under low brows, black with night,
Rayed out at times a dangerous light;
The sharp heat-lightnings of her face
Presaging ill to him whom Fate
Condemned to share her love or hate.
A woman tropical, intense
In thought and act, in soul and sense,
She blended in a like degree
The vixen and the devotee.
Revealing with each freak or feint
    The temper of Petruchio's Kate,
The raptures of Siena's saint.
Her tapering hand and rounded wrist
Had facile power to form a fist;
The warm, dark languish of her eyes
Was never safe from wrath's surprise.
Brows saintly calm and lips devout
Knew every change of scowl and pout;
And the sweet voice had notes more high

And shrill for social battle-cry.

Since then what old cathedral town
Has missed her pilgrim staff and gown,
What convent-gate has held its lock
Against the challenge of her knock!
Through Smyra's plague-hushed thoroughfares,
Up sea-set Malta's rocky stairs,
Grayy olive slopes of hills that hem
Thy tombs and shrines, Jerusalem,
Or startling on her desert throne
The crazy Queen of Lebanon
With claims fantastic as her own,
Her tireless feet have held their way;

And still, unrestful, bowed, and gray,
She watches under Eastern skies,
    With hope each day renewed and fresh,
    The Lord's quick coming in the flesh
Whereof she dreams and prophesies!

Where'er her troubled path may be,
    The Lord's sweet pity with her go!
The outward wayward life we see,
    The hidden springs we may not know.
Nor is it given us to discern
    What threads the fatal sisters spun,
    Through what ancestral years has run
The sorrow with the woman born,
What forged her cruel chain of moods,
What set her feet in solitudes,
    And held the love within her mute,
What mingled madness in the blood,
    A life-long discord and annoy,
    Water of tears with oil of joy,
And hid within the folded bud
    Perversities of flower and fruit.
It is not ours to separate
The tangled skein of will and fate,

To show what metes and bounds should stand
Upon the soul's debatable land,
And between choice and Providence
Divide the circle of events;
But He who knows our frame is just,
Merciful and compassionate,
And full of sweet assurances
And hope for all the language is,
That He remembereth we are dust!

At last the great logs, crumbling low,
Sent out a dull and duller glow,
The bull's-eye watch that hung in view,
Ticking its weary circuit through,
Pointed with mutely warning sign
Its black hand to the hour of nine.

That sign the pleasant circle broke:
My uncle ceased his pipe to smoke,
Knocked from its bowl the refuse gray,
And laid it tenderly away;
Then roused himself to safely cover
The dull red brands with ashes over.
And while, with care, our mother laid
The work aside, her steps she stayed
One moment, seeking to express
Her grateful sense of happiness
For food and shelter, warmth and health
And love's contentment more than wealth,
With simple wishes (not the weak,
Vain prayers which no fulfilment seek,
But such as warm the generous heart,
O'er-prompt to do with Heaven its part)
That none might lack, that bitter night.
For bread and clothing, warmth and light.

Within our beds awhile we heard
The wind that round the gables roared,
With now and then a ruder shock,

Which made our very bedsteads rock.
We heard the loosened clapboards tost,
The board-nails snapping in the frost;
And on us, through the unplastered wall,
Felt the light sifted snow-flakes fall.
But sleep stole on, as sleep will do
When hearts are light and life is new;
Faint and more faint the murmurs grew,
Till in the summer-land of dreams
They softened to the sound of streams,
Low stir of leaves, and dip of oars,
And lapsing waves on quiet shores.

Next morn we wakened with the shout
Of merry voices high and clear;
And saw the teamsters drawing near
To break the drifted highways out.
Down the long hillside treading slow
We saw the half-buried oxen go,
Shaking the snow from heads uptost,
Their straining nostrils white with frost.
Before our door the straggling train
Drew up, an added team to gain.
The elders threshed their hands a-cold,
    Passed with cider-mugs, their jokes
    From lip to lip; the younger folks
Down the loose snow-banks, wrestling, rolled,
Then toiled again the cavalcade
    O'er windy hill, through clogged ravine,
    And woodland paths that wound between
Low drooping pine-boughs winter-weighed.
From every barn a team afoot,
At every house a new recruit,
Where, drawn by Nature's subtlest law,
Haply the watchful young men saw
Sweet doorway pictures of the curls
And curious eyes of merry girls,
Lifting their hands in mock defence
Against the snow-ball's compliments,

And reading in each missive tost
The charm with Eden never lost.

We heard once more the sleigh-bell's sound;
    And, following where the teamsters led,
The wise old Doctor went his round,
Just pausing at our door to say,
In the brief autocratic way
Of one who, prompt at Duty's call,
Was free to urge her claim on all,
    That some poor neighbor sick abed
At night our mother's aid would need.
For, one in generous thought and deed,
    What mattered in the sufferer's sight
    The Quaker matron's inward light,
The Doctor's mail of Calvin's creed?
All hearts confess the saints elect
    Who, twain in faith, in love agree,
And melt not in an acid sect
The Christian pearl of charity!

So days went on: a week had passed
Since the great world was heard from last.
The Almanac we studied o'er,
Read and reread our little store
Of books and pamphlets, scarce a score;
One harmless novel, mostly hid
From younger eyes, a book forbid,
And poetry, (or good or bad,
A single book was all we had,)
Where Ellwood's meek, drab-skirted Muse,
    A stranger to the heathen Nine,
    Sang, with a somewhat nasal whine
The wars of David and the Jews.
At last the floundering carrier bore
The village paper to our door
Lo! broadening outward as we read,
To warmer zones the horizon spread;
In panoramic length unrolled

We saw the marvels that it told.
Before us passed the painted Creeks,
   And daft McGregor on his raids
   In Costa Rica's everglades.
And up Taygetos winding slow
Rode Ypsilanti's Mainote Greeks,
A Turk's head at each saddle-bow!
Welcome to us its week-old news,
Its corner for the rustic Muse,
   Its monthly gauge of snow and rain,
Its record, mingling in a breath
The wedding bell and dirge of death;
Jest, anecdote, and love-lorn tale,
The latest culprit sent to jail;
Its hue and cry of stolen and lost,
Its vendue sales and goods at cost,
   And traffic calling loud for gain.
We felt the stir of hall and street,
The pulse of life that round us beat;
The chill embargo of the snow
Was melted in the genial glow;
Wide swung again our ice-locked door,
And all the world was ours once more!

Clasp, Angel of the backward look
   And folded wings of ashen gray
   And voice of echoes far away,
The brazen covers of thy book;
The weird palimpsest old and vast,
Wherein thou hid'st the spectral past;
Where, closely mingling, pale and glow
The characters of joy and woe;
The monographs of outlived years,
Or smile-illumed or dim with tears,
   Green hills of life that slope to death,
And haunts of home, whose vistaed trees
Shade off to mournful cypresses
   With the white amaranths underneath.
Even while I look, I can but heed

The restless sands' incessant fall,
Importunate hours that hours succeed,
Each clamorous with its own sharp need,
    And duty keeping pace with all.
Shut down and clasp the heavy lids;
I hear again the voice that bids
The dreamer leave his dream midway
For larger hopes and graver fears:
Life greatens in these later years,
The century's aloe flowers to-day!

Yet, haply, in some lull of life,
Some Truce of God which breaks its strife
The worldling's eyes shall gather dew,
    Dreaming in throngful city ways
Of winter joys his boyhood knew;
And dear and early friends—the few
Who yet remain—shall pause to view
    These Flemish pictures of old days;
Sit with me by the homestead hearth,
And stretch the hands of memory forth
    To warm them at the wood-fire's blaze!
And thanks untraced to lips unknown
Shall greet me like the odors blown
From unseen meadows newly mown,
Or lilies floating in some pond,
Wood-fringed, the wayside gaze beyond;
The traveller owns the grateful sense
Of sweetness near, he knows not whence,
And, pausing, takes with forehead bare
The benediction of the air.

HERMAN MELVILLE [1819-1891]

Herman Melville was born into a prestigious New York City family. He was a direct descendent of Thomas Melville, a military officer of the American Revolution known for his activity in connection with the Boston Tea Party. In 1830, however, his father, Alan Melville, went bankrupt, and moved the family to Albany, New York. These difficulties prompted Melville to withdraw from the Albany Academy and to take the position of a local bank clerk; later, he worked winters in a hat store and summers on a farm. In his spare hours, he studied at the Albany Classical School. But this life did not suit him, and in June of 1839, after a brief stint as a school teacher, he departed for Liverpool, England.

He spent several months in Liverpool before returning to Lansingburgh, New York, where his mother lived. He taught school once more but soon resolved to go to sea again. On January 3, 1841, he set sail from New Bedford, Massachusetts, on the whaling ship *Acushnet;* he would be gone for almost four years. After several months, Melville became tired of the inhuman conditions imposed by his superiors, and upon arrival to the Marquesa Islands in the South Pacific, he jumped ship. Soon he was captured by a tribe of cannibals, the Taipis, but was not harmed; instead, he was treated as an honored guest and was cordially extended every privilege. His novel *Typee* (1845), is based on this experience.

Eventually, Melville came to need medical attention for an infected leg and was, therefore, forced to return to civilization. He left the South Pacific as a sailor on the *Lucy Ann*, an Australian whaler bound for Tahiti. There, he was imprisoned by the British Consul for refusing to continue duties aboard ship. He escaped with a friend to the neighboring island Eimeo where he spent a month before joining the Nantucket whaler *Charles and Henry*. He arrived in Hawaii in April 1843, and worked as a clerk in Honolulu, before being pressed into naval service on the frigate, *United States*. However, it was only a year later that he landed in Boston and his seafaring years finally came to an end.

Upon returning home, Melville began writing *Typee* and thinking seriously of a career as a novelist. In 1846, he wrote *Omoo*. Together with *Typee*, this proved to be a resounding commercial success; it was written in the style of a travelogue which was very popular at the time. In 1847, he married Elizabeth Shaw, daughter of Lemuel Shaw, the Chief Justice of Massachusetts. They lived for three years in York City before moving to the Berkshires in 1850. There, Melville began what was to be his masterpiece and one of the greatest American novels of all time, *Moby Dick* (1851). This work, however, and the one that followed, *Pierre* (1852), were commercial failures which initially met serious disapproval from the critics. Melville was torn between the demands of the public and his inner quest for artistic ideals. Between 1853 and 1856, he concentrated on writing essays and short stories for periodicals; *Israel Potter,* a historical novel, was serialized in 1854. After the publication of his last novel, *The Confidence Man* (1857), Melville seemed near a breakdown. He was ordered to take a trip abroad for his health; financed by his father-in-law, he toured Greece, Constantinople, Egypt, Italy and England.

From 1859 on, he devoted himself almost exclusively to poetry. Although in recent years his verse has attracted a good deal of attention, it was mainly overlooked at the time. Melville published three volumes of verse and a six-hundred page narrative poem, *Clarel* (1876). Much of his poetry has been lost; much of it he himself destroyed. In 1866, he was appointed Deputy Inspector of Customs; a year later, his son, Malcolm, committed suicide. In 1886, his wife received a legacy that finally allowed him to retire.

Now regarded as one of the foremost figures in American literature, Melville died in 1891 obscure and all but forgotten. At the time of his death he had returned to writing fiction. His well-known short story "Billy Bud" dates from this late period; it was published posthumously in 1924.

L'envoi
The Return of the Sire de Nesle
A.D. 16—

My towers at last! These rovings end,
   Their thirst is slaked in larger dearth:
The yearning infinite recoils,
   For terrible is earth.

Kaf thrusts his snouted crags through fog:
Araxes swells beyond his span,
And knowledge poured by pilgrimage
Overflows the banks of man.

But thou, my stay, thy lasting love
One lonely good, let this but be!
Weary to view the wide world's swarm,
   But blest to fold but thee.

Stonewall Jackson
Mortally Wounded At Chancellorsville
[May, 1863]

The Man who fiercest charged in fight,
   Whose sword and prayer were long—
      Stonewall!
   Even him who stoutly stood for Wrong,
How can we praise? Yet coming days
   Shall not forget him with this song.

Dead is the Man whose Cause is dead,
   Vainly he died and set his seal—
      Stonewall!

Earnest in error, as we feel;
True to the thing he deemed was due,
True as John Brown or steel.

Relentlessly he routed us;
    But *we* relent, for he is low—
        Stonewall!
    Justly his fame we outlaw; so
We drop a tear on the bold Virginian's bier,
Because no wreath we owe.

The Aeolian Harp

At The Surf Inn

List the harp in window wailing
    Stirred by fitful gales from sea:
Shrieking up in mad crescendo—
    Dying down in plaintive key!

Listen: less a strain ideal
    Than Ariel's rendering of the Real.
What that Real is, let hint
    A picture stamped in memory's mint.

Braced well up, with beams aslant,
Betwixt the continents sails the *Phocion,*
For Baltimore bound from Alicant.
Blue breezy skies white fleeces fleck
Over the chill blue white-capped ocean:
From yard-arm comes—"Wreck ho, a wreck!"

Dismasted and adrift,
Long time a thing forsaken:
Overwashed by every wave
Like the slumbering kraken:

Heedless if the billow roar,
Oblivious of the lull,
Leagues and legues from shoal or shore,
It swims—a levelled hull:
Bulwarks gone—a shaven wreck,
Nameless, and a grass-green deck.
A lumberman: perchance, in hold
Prostrate pines with hemlocks rolled.

It has drifted, waterlogged,
Till by trailing weeds beclogged:
    Drifted, drifted, day by day,
    Pilotless on pathless way.

It has drifted till each plank
Is oozy as the oyster-bank:
    Drifted, drifted, night by night,
    Craft that never shows a light:
Nor ever, to prevent worse knell,
Tolls in fog the warning bell.

From collision never shrinking,
Drive what may through darksome smother:
Saturate, but never sinking,
Fatal only to the *other!*
    Deadlier than the sunken reef
    Since still the snare it shifteth,
        Torpid in dumb ambuscade
    Waylaying it drifteth.

        O, the sailors— O, the sails!
        O, the lost crews never heard of!
        Well the harp of Ariel wails
        Thoughts that tongue can tell no word of!

The Portent [1859]

Hanging from the beam,
    Slowly swaying (such the law),
Gaunt the shadow on your green,
    Shenandoah!
The cut is on the crown
(Lo, John Brown),
and the stabs shall heal no more.

Hidden in the cap
    Is the anguish none can draw;
So the future veils its face,
    Shenandoah!
But the streaming beard is shown
(Weird John Brown),
The meteor of the war.

The Conflict of Convictions [1860-1]

On starry heights
  A bugle wails the long recall;
Derision stirs the deep abyss,
  Heaven's ominous silence over all.
Return, return, O eager Hope,
  And face man's latter fall.
Events, they make the dreamers quail;
  Satan's old age is strong and hale,
A disciplined captain, gray in skill,
  And Raphael a white enthusiast still;
Dashed aims, at which Christ's martyrs pale,
  Shall Mammon's slaves fulfill?

      (Dismantle the fort,
      Cut down the fleet—
      Battle no more shall be!
      While the fields for fight in æons to come
      Congeal beneath the sea.)

The terrors of truth and dart of death
  To faith alike are vain:
Though comets, gone a thousand years,
    Return again,
Patient she stands—she can no more—
And waits, nor heeds she waxes hoar.

      (At a stony gate,
      A statue of stone,
      Weed overgrown—
      Long 'twill wait!)

But God his former mind retains,
  Confirms his old decree;
The generations are inured to pains,
  And strong Necessity
Surges, and heaps Time's strand with wrecks.

The People spread like a weedy grass,
The thing they will they bring to pass,
And prosper to the apoplex.
The rout it herds around the heart,
    The ghost is yielded in the gloom:
Kings wag their heads—Now save thyself
    Who wouldst rebuild the world in bloom.

> *(Tide-mark*
> *And top of the ages' strife,*
> *Verge where they called the world to come,*
> *The last advance of life—*
> *Ha ha, the rust on the Iron Dome!)*

Nay, but revere the hid event;
    In the cloud a sword is girded on,
I mark a twinkling in the tent
    Of Michael the warrior one.
Senior wisdom suits not now,
The light is on the youthful brow.

> *(Ay, in caves the miner see:*
> *His forehead bears a blinking light;*
> *Darkness so he feebly braves—*
> *A meagre wight!)*

But He who rules is old—is old;
Ah! faith is warm, but heaven with age is cold.

> *(Ho, ho, ho ho,*
> *The cloistered doubt*
> *Of olden times*
> *Is blurted out!)*

The Ancient of Days forever is young,
    Forever the scheme of Nature thrives;
I know a wind in purpose strong—
    It spins *against* the way it drives.
What if the gulfs their slimed foundations bare?

So deep must the stones be hurled
Whereon the throes of ages rear
The final empire and the happier world.

> *(The poor old Past,*
> *The Future's slave,*
> *She drudged through pain and crime*
> *To bring about the blissful Prime,*
> *Then—perished. There's a grave!)*

Power unanointed may come—
Dominion (unsought by the free)
    And the Iron Dome,

Stronger for stress and strain,
Fling her huge shadow athwart the main;
But the Founders' dream shall flee.
Age after age shall be
As age after age has been,
(From man's changeless heart their way they win):
And death be busy with all who strive—
Death, with silent negative.

YEA AND NAY—
EACH HATH HIS SAY;
BUT GOD HE KEEPS THE MIDDLE WAY.
NONE WAS BY
WHEN HE SPREAD THE SKY;
WISDOM IS VAIN, AND PROPHESY.

America

I

Where the wings of a sunny Dome expand
I saw a Banner in gladsome air—
Starry, like Berenice's Hair—
Afloat in broadened bravery there;
With undulating long-drawn flow,
As rolled Brazilian billows go
Voluminously o'er the Line.
The Land reposed in peace below;
   The children in their glee
Were folded to the exulting heart
   Of young Maternity.

II

Later, and it streamed in fight
   When tempest mingled with the fray,
And over the spear-point of the shaft
   I saw the ambiguous lightning play.
Valor with Valor strove, and died:
Fierce was Despair, and cruel was Pride;
And the lorn Mother speechless stood,
Pale at the fury of her brood.

III

Yet later, and the silk did wind
    Her fair cold form;
Little availed the shining shroud,
   Though ruddy in hue, to cheer or warm.
A watcher looked upon her low, and said—
She sleeps, but sleeps, she is not dead.
   But in that sleep contortion showed
The terror of the vision there—
   A silent vision unavowed,
Revealing earth's foundation bare,
    And Gorgon in her hidden place.
   It was a thing of fear to see

So foul a dream upon so fair a face,
And the dreamer lying in that starry shroud.

IV

But from the trance she sudden broke—
    The trance, or death into promoted life;
At her feet a shivered yoke,
And in her aspect turned to heaven
    No trace of passion or of strife—
A clear calm look. It spake of pain,
But such as purifies from stain—
Sharp pangs that never come again—
    And triumph repressed by knowledge meet,
Power dedicate, and hope grown wise,
    And youth matured for age's seat—
Law on her brow and empire in her eyes.
    So, she, with graver air and lifted flag;
While the shadow, chased by light,
Fled along the far-drawn height,
    And left her on the crag.

On the Slain Collegians

Youth is the time when hearts are large,
          And stirring wars
Appeal to the spirit which appeals in turn
          To the blade it draws.
If woman incite, and duty show
          (Though made the mask of Cain),
Or whether it be Truth's sacred cause,
          Who can aloof remain
That shares youth's ardor, uncooled by the snow
          Of wisdom or sordid gain?

The liberal arts and nurture sweet
Which give his gentleness to man—
          Train him to honor, lend him grace
Through bright examples meet—
That culture which makes never wan
With underminings deep, but holds
          The surface still, its fitting place,
          And so gives sunniness to the face
And bravery to the heart; what troops
          Of generous boys in happiness thus bred—
          Saturnians through life's Tempe led,
Went from the North and came from the South,
With golden mottoes in the mouth,
          To lie down midway on a bloody bed.

Woe for the homes of the North,
And woe for the seats of the South:
All who felt life's spring in prime,
And were swept by the wind of their place and time—
          All lavish hearts, on whichever side,
Of birth urbane or courage high,
Armed them for the stirring wars—
Armed them—some to die.
          Apollo-like in pride,
Each would slay his Python—caught

The maxims in his temple taught—
  Aflame with sympathies whose blaze
Perforce enwrapped him—social laws,
  Friendship and kin, and by-gone days—
Vows, kisses—every heart unmoors,
And launches into the seas of wars.
What could they else—North or South?
Each went forth with blessings given
By priests and mothers in the name of Heaven:
  And honor in both was chief.
Warred one for Right, and one for Wrong?

So be it: but they both were young—
  Each grape to his cluster clung,
  All their elegies are sung.

The anguish of maternal hearts
  Must search for balm divine;
But well the striplings bore their fated parts
  (The heavens all parts assign)—
Never felt life's care or cloy.
Each bloomed and died an unabated Boy;
Nor dreamed what death was—thought it mere
Sliding into some vernal sphere.
They knew the joy, but leaped the grief,
Like plants that flower ere come the leaf—
Which storms lay low in kindly doom,
And kill them in their flush of bloom.

Malvern Hill [1862]

Ye elms that wave on Malvern Hill
    In prime of morn and May,
Recall ye how McClellan's men
    Here stood at bay?

While deep within yon forest dim
    Our rigid comrades lay—
Some with the cartridge in their mouth,
Others with fixed arms lifted South—
        Invoking so
The cypress glades? Ah wilds of woe!

The spires of Richmond, late beheld
    Through rifts in musket-haze,
Were closed from view in clouds of dust
    On leaf-walled ways,
Where streamed our wagons in caravan;
    And the Seven Nights and Days
Of march and fast, retreat and fight,
Pinched our grimed faces to ghastly plight—
        Does the elm wood
Recall the haggard beards of blood?

The battle-smoked flag, with stars eclipsed,
    We followed (it never fell!)—
In silence husbanded our strength—
        Received their yell;
Till on this slope we patient turned
    With cannon ordered well;
Reverse we proved was not defeat:
But ah, the sod what thousands meet!—
        Does Malvern Wood
Bethink itself, and muse and brood?

We elms of Malvern Hill
    Remember every thing;

But sap the twig will fill:
Wag the world how it will,
  Leaves must be green in Spring.

Art [1891]

In placid hours well-pleased we dream
Of many a brave unbodied scheme.
But form to lend, pulsed life create,
What unlike things must meet and mate:
A flame to melt—a wind to freeze;
Sad patience—joyous energies;
Humility—yet pride and scorn;
Instinct and study; love and hate;
Audacity—reverence. These must mate,
And fuse with Jacob's mystic heart,
To wrestle with the angel—Art.

After The Pleasure Party [1891]

Lines Traced Under an Image of Amor Threatening

Fear me, virgin whosoever
Taking pride from love exempt,
Fear me, slighted. Never, never
Brave me, nor my fury tempt:
Downy wings, but wroth they beat
Tempest even in reason's seat.

Behind the house the upland falls
With many an odorous tree—

White marbles gleaming through green halls,
Terrace by terrace, down and down,
And meets the starlit Mediterranean Sea.

'Tis Paradise. In such an hour
Some pangs that rend might take release.
Nor less perturbed who keeps this bower
Of balm, nor finds balsamic peace?
From whom the passionate words in vent
After long revery's discontent?

Tired of the homeless deep,
Look how their flight yon hurrying billows urge,
Hitherward but to reap
Passive repulse from the iron-bound verge!
Insensate, can they never know
'Tis mad to wreck the impulsion so?

An art of memory is, they tell:
But to forget! forget the glade
Wherein Fate sprung Love's ambuscade,
To flout pale years of cloistral life

On her—to fire this petty hell,
His softened glance how moistly fell!
The cheat! on briars her buds were strung;
And wiles peeped forth from mien how meek.
The innocent bare-foot! young, so young!
To girls, strong man's a novice weak.
To tell such beads! And more remain,
Sad rosary of belittling pain.

When after lunch and sallies gay,
Like the Decameron folk we lay
In sylvan groups; and I—let be!
O, dreams he, can he dream that one
Because not roseate feels no sun?
The plain lone bramble thrills with Spring
As much as vines that grapes shall bring.

Me now fair studies charm no more.
Shall great thoughts writ, or high themes sung
Damask wan cheeks—unlock his arm
About some radiant ninny flung?
How glad with all my starry lore,
I'd buy the veriest wanton's rose
Would but my bee therein repose.

Could I remake me! or set free
The sexless bound in sex, then plunge
Deeper than Sappho, in a lunge
Piercing Pan's paramount mystery!
For, Nature, in no shallow surge
Against thee either sex may urge,
Why hast thou made us but in halves—
Co-relatives? This makes us slaves.
If these co-relatives never meet
Self-hood itself seems incomplete.
And such the dicing of blind fate
Few matching halves here meet and mate.
What Cosmic jest or Anarch blunder
The human integral clove asunder
And shied the fractions through life's gate?

Ye stars that long your votary knew
Rapt in her vigil, see me here!
Whither is gone the spell ye threw
When rose before me Cassiopea?
Usurped on by love's stronger reign—
But lo, your very selves do wane:
Light breaks—truth breaks! Silvered no more,
But chilled by dawn that brings the gale
Shivers yon bramble above the vale,
And disillusion opens all the shore.

One knows not if Urania yet
The pleasure-party may forget;
Or whether she lived down the strain
Of turbulent heart and rebel brain;

For Amor so resents a slight,
And her's had been such haught disdain,
He long may wreak his boyish spite,
And boy-like, little reck the pain.

   One knows not, no. But late in Rome
(For queens discrowned a congruous home)
Entering Albani's porch she stood
Fixed by an antique pagan stone
Colossal carved. No anchorite seer,
Not Thomas a Kempis, monk austere,
Religious more are in their tone;
Yet far, how far from Christian heart
That form august of heathen Art.
Swayed by its influence, long she stood,
Till surged emotion seething down,
She rallied and this mood she won:

   Languid in frame for me,
To-day by Mary's convent shrine,
Touching by her picture's moving plea
In that poor nerveless hour of mine,

I mused—A wanderer still must grieve.
Half I resolved to kneel and believe,
Believe and submit, the veil take on.
But thee, armed Virgin! less benign,
Thee now I invoke, thou mightier one.
Helmeted woman—if such term
Befit thee, far from strife
Of that which makes the sexual feud
And clogs the aspirant life—
O self-reliant, strong and free,
Thou in whom power and peace unite,
Transcender! raise me up to thee,
Raise me and arm me!

                Fond appeal.
For never passion peace shall bring,

Nor Art inanimate for long
Inspire. Nothing may help or heal
While Amor incensed remembers wrong.
Vindictive, not himself he'll spare;
For scope to give his vengeance play
Himself he'll blaspheme and betray.

Then for Urania, virgins everywhere,
O pray! Example take too, and have care.

Pebbles [1888]

I

Though the Clerk of the Weather insist,
    And lay down the weather-law,
Pintado and gannet they wist
That the winds blow whither they list
    In tempest or flaw.

II

Old are the creeds, but stale the schools,
    Revamped as the mode may veer,
But Orm from the schools to the beaches strays,
And, finding a Conch hoar with time, he delays
    And reverent lifts it to ear.
That Voice, pitched in far monotone,
    Shall it swerve? shall it deviate ever?
The Seas have inspired it, and Truth—
    Truth, varying from sameness never.

III

In hollows of the liquid hills
    Where the long Blue Ridges run,

The flattery of no echo thrills,
   For echo the seas have none;
Nor aught that gives man back man's strain—
The hope of his heart, the dream in his brain.

IV

On ocean where the embattled fleets repair,
Man, suffering inflictor, sails on sufferance there.

V

Implacable I, the old implacable Sea:
   Implacable most when most I smile serene—
Pleased, not appeased, by myriad wrecks in me.

VI

Curled in the comb of yon billow Andean,
   Is it the Dragon's heaven-challenging crest?
Elemental mad ramping of ravening waters—
   Yet Christ on the Mount, and the dove in her nest!

VII

Healed of my hurt, I laud the inhuman Sea—
Yea, bless the Angels Four that there convene;

For healed I am even by their pitiless breath
Distilled in wholesome dew named rosmarine.

The Berg [1888]

(A Dream)

I saw a ship of martial build
(Her standards set, her brave apparel on)
Directed as by madness mere
Against a stolid iceberg steer,
Nor budge it, though the infatuate ship went down.
The impact made huge ice-cubes fall
Sullen, in tons that crashed the deck;

But that one avalanche was all—
No other movement save the foundering wreck.

Along the spurs of ridges pale,
Not any slenderest shaft and frail,
A prism over glass-green gorges lone,
Toppled; nor lace of traceries fine,
Nor pendant drops in grot or mine
Were jarred, when the stunned ship went down.
Nor sole the gulls in cloud that wheeled
Circling one snow-flanked peak afar,
But nearer fowl the floes that skimmed
And crystal beaches, felt no jar.
No thrill transmitted stirred the lock
Of jack-straw needle-ice at base;
Towers undermined by waves—the block
Atilt impending—kept their place.
Seals, dozing sleek on sliddery ledges
Slipt never, when by loftier edges
Through very inertia overthrown,
The impetuous ship in bafflement went down.

Hard Berg (methought), so cold, so vast,
With mortal damps self-overcast;
Exhaling still thy dankish breath—
Adrift dissolving, bound for death;

Though lumpish thou, a lumbering one—
A lumbering lubbard loitering slow,
Impingers rue thee and go down,
Sounding thy precipice below,
Nor stir the slimy slug that sprawls
Along thy dead indifference of walls.

Shiloh
A Requiem
[April, 1862]

SKIMMING lightly, wheeling still,
    The swallows fly low
Over the field in clouded days,
    The forest-field of Shiloh—
Over the field where April rain
Solaced the parched one stretched in pain
Through the pause of night
That followed the Sunday fight
    Around the church of Shiloh—
The church so lone, the log-built one,
That echoed to many a parting groan
        And natural prayer
    Of dying foemen mingled there—
Foemen at morn, but friends at eve—
    Fame or country least their care:
(What like a bullet can undeceive!)
    But now they lie low,
While over them the swallows skim,
And all is hushed at Shiloh.

Pontoosuce

Crowning a bluff where gleams the lake below,
Some pillared pines in well-spaced order stand
And like an open temple show.
And here in best of seasons bland,
Autumnal noon-tide, I look out
From dusk arcades on sunshine all about.

Beyond the Lake, in upland cheer
Fields, pastoral fields, and barns appear,
They skirt the hills where lonely roads
Revealed in links thro' tiers of woods
Wind up to indistinct abodes
And faery-peopled neighborhoods;
While further fainter mountains keep
Hazed in romance impenetrably deep.

Look, corn in stacks, on many a farm,
And orchards ripe in languorous charm,
As dreamy Nature, feeling sure
Of all her genial labor done,
And the last mellow fruitage won,
Would idle out her term mature;
Reposing like a thing reclined
In kinship with man's meditative mind.

For me, within the brown arcade—
Rich life, methought; sweet here in shade
And pleasant abroad in air!—But, nay,
A counter thought intrusive played,
A thought as old as thought itself,
And who shall lay it on the shelf!—
I felt the beauty bless the day
In opulence of autumn's dower;
But evanescence will not stay!
A year ago was such an hour,
As this, which but foreruns the blast

Shall sweep these live leaves to the dead leaves past.

All dies!—

    I stood in revery long.
Then, to forget death's ancient wrong,
I turned me in the brown arcade,
And there by chance in lateral glade
I saw low tawny mounds in lines
Relics of trunks of stately pines
Ranked erst in colonnades where, lo!
Erect succeeding pillars show!

    All dies! and not alone
The aspiring trees and men and grass;
The poet's forms of beauty pass,
And noblest deeds they are undone.

All dies!

The workman dies, and after him, the work;
Like to these pines whose graves I trace,
Statue and statuary fall upon their face:
In very amaranths the worm doth lurk,
Even stars, Chaldaeans say, fade from the starry space.
Andes and Apalachee tell
Of havoc ere our Adam fell,
And present Nature as a moss doth show
On the ruins of the Nature of the aeons of long ago.

But look—and hark!

    Adown the glade,
Where light and shadow sport at will,
Who cometh vocal, and arrayed
As in the first pale tints of morn—
So pure, rose-clear, and fresh and chill!
Some ground-pine sprigs her brow adorn,

The earthy rootlets tangled clinging.
Over tufts of moss which dead things made,
Under vital twigs which danced or swayed,
Along she floats, and lightly singing:
"Dies, all dies!
The grass it dies, but in vernal rain
Up it springs and it lives again;
Over and over, again and again
It lives, it dies and it lives again.
Who sighs that all dies?
Summer and winter, and pleasure and pain
And everything everywhere in God's reign,
They end, and anon they begin again:
Wane and wax, wax and wane:
Over and over and over again
End, ever end, and begin again—
End, ever end, and forever and ever begin again!"

She ceased, and nearer slid, and hung
In dewy guise; then softlier sung:

"Since light and shade are equal set
And all revolves, nor more ye know;
Ah, why should tears the pale cheek fret
For aught that waneth here below.
Let go, let go!"

With that, her warm lips thrilled me through,
She kissed me, while her chaplet cold
Its rootlets brushed against my brow
With all their humid clinging mould.
She vanished, leaving fragrant breath
And warmth and chill of wedded life and death.

WALT WHITMAN [1819-1892]

Walt Whitman was born to poorly educated parents in rural Huntington, Long Island. Although his family eventually moved to Brooklyn, he often visited the old location. He had a sentimental attachment to the place and a profound respect for its history. He frequently referred to it by the Indian name, "Paumanok." Whitman is one of America's truly great poets. His work exhibits a bold, free-flowing poetic style which is readily associated with the sentiments of democratic ideology.

Although the poet's early years were spent at hard work, they did not seem to offer much promise in terms of a literary career. In the first place, Whitman never completed his education; he attended public school in Brooklyn and, at age eleven, made a decision to abandon formal studies in favor of work as an office boy at local newspapers and publishers. Nevertheless, as an eager young man, his thirst for learning did not diminish, and he continued to pursue personal interests, especially in the field of literature and journalism. Eventually, he was able to take on serious responsibilities as editor; thus, from 1846-48 he worked for the *Brooklyn Eagle,* and in 1851 he joined the staff of the *Crescent* in New Orleans. During these years, he managed to publish some verse as well as prose. But none of this work, including the novel *Franklin Evans* was met with particular success. Therefore, by the time he moved back to Brooklyn, he was still a simple professional whose deep personal aspirations in the field of literature had failed to show positive results.

The turning point in Whitman's career, however, was soon to follow. When he returned to his parents home, it was, perhaps, a sense of frustration that inspired him to adopt a different way of life and to earn a living as a carpenter. In this way, he felt, one could end an official involvement with literature in order to pursue creative interests independently. In fact, in his case, this decision proved correct, and by 1855 he was able to produce the first edition of his famous collection of poems entitled *Leaves of Grass.* Interestingly enough, the book, published anonymously at the author's expense, appeared with a frontispiece depicting the rugged-looking, bearded poet in work clothes. Although the publication was initially a commercial failure and was not widely appreciated, its overwhelming importance gradually became self-evident; it signified the beginning of a prodigious career by one of the most ingenius of all American poets. Fortunately, at the time, a few individuals recognized the fact. Among these was Ralph Waldo Emerson, to whom Whitman had sent a copy of the publication; in a letter of reply, he extolled *Leaves of Grass* as "the most extraordinary piece of wit and wisdom that America has yet contributed." Needless to say, such recognition, from a towering literary figure of the period did much to encourage the hitherto unknown poet.

Over the years, critics have offered various explanations for this enigmatic turn of events. What prompted Whitman's unexpected leap from journeyman newspaper editor to major writer? Had Whitman fallen in love? Or, was his work a response to private, mystical feelings? Furthermore, were there other poets who had inspired Whitman to suddenly develop such poetic mastery? All of these are legitimate questions. But the fact remains that, beginning with *Leaves of Grass,* Whitman was destined to continue writing in a unique, personal style. The robust abandon of his writing can be linked to special qualities of Hebraic poetry as found in the Bible. This approach, in particular, was unknown at the time; it allowed the poet to treat subjects that others considered inappropriate and prosaic. Indeed, at one point, Whitman was dismissed from a job at the Department of the Interior because the Secretary felt that his publications were indecent. The undaunted genius, however, continued rewriting and expanding his original work. As a result, there emerged thirteen editions of *Leaves of Grass* during the poet's lifetime, and the work is now universally recognized as a landmark in the history of American literature.

The events of the Civil War signify another important phase in Whitman's life. Despite his rough appearance, the poet had a sensitive and compassionate personality. During the war, therefore, he could not by-pass the dreadful sight of bloodshed and became a nurse. His active involvement was first called upon in 1862, when he journeyed to Washington to care for his wounded brother, George. This, in turn, inspired him for the coming years; he was to remain in an army hospital until the end of the war, caring for the wounded and assisting in numerous activities including surgery. Whitman was acutely aware of the historical significance of events around him; he firmly believed that the outcome of suffering will have a lasting impact on the future of the great American nation and that, as a result, his duty as a medical aide was to help victims from *both* sides of the front. His poetry, written after the war, reflects these idealistic sentiments. In particular, one might cite the small collection entitled *Drum-Taps* (1865) and then, of course, the famous elegy on the death of Abraham Lincoln, *"When Lilacs Last in the Dooryard Bloom'd".*

By the late 1860's, Whitman had acquired considerable reknown, and critics in England as well as the United States began to acknowledge the importance of his startling literary output. On the one hand, there were figures such as Henry James, W.D. Howells, Matthew Arnold and others who were extremely critical; they believed that Whitman had taken unnecessary liberty with his poetry and had shattered the basic premises of a lofty, exalted genre. On the other hand, there were others such as the English critic J.A. Symonds, the poets Algernon Swinburne, Dante Gabriel Rossetti, and the reknowned Russian writer, Ivan Turgenev; these celebrated personalities were deeply impressed and regarded Whitman as a great American bard. Eventually, Henry James also became an avid supporter. Despite difficulties with the Secretary at the Department of Interior, during these years Whitman managed to continue working for the government and held a position in the office of the Attorney General.

Then, in 1873, Whitman suffered a stroke which left him partially disabled. He retired to Camden, New Jersey, where life was suitably quiet and he could continue writing at a leisurely pace. Surrounded by a growing number of admirers, he published further editions of *Leaves of Grass* as well as an anecdotal autobiography entitled *Specimen Days* (1882). Subsequent strokes, however, continued to limit his creativity, and he died in 1892 at the age of seventy-three.

*When I Heard The
Learned Astronomer*

When I heard the learned astronomer,
When the proofs, the figures, were ranged in columns before
    me,
When I was shown the charts and diagrams, to add, divide,
    and measure them,
When I sitting heard the astronomer where he lectured with
    much applause in the lecture room,
How soon unaccountable I became tired and sick,
Till rising and gliding out I wandered off by myself,
In the mystical moist night air, and from time to time,
Looked up in perfect silence at the stars.

There Was a Child Went Forth

There was a child went forth every day,
And the first object he look'd upon, that object he became,
And that object became part of him for the day or a
        certain part of the day,
Or for many years or stretching cycles of years.

The early lilacs became part of this child,
And grass and white and red morning-glories, and white
        and red clover, and the song of the phoebe-bird,
And the Third-month lambs and the sow's pink-faint litter,
        and the mare's foal and the cow's calf,
And the noisy brood of the barnyard or by the mire of the
        pond-side,
And the fish suspending themselves so curiously below
        there, and the beautiful curious liquid,
And the water-plants with their graceful flat heads, all
        became part of him.

The field-sprouts of Fourth-month and Fifth-month be-
      came part of him,
Winter-grain sprouts and those of the light-yellow corn,
      and the esculent roots of the garden,
And the apple-trees cover'd with blossoms and the fruit
      afterward, and wood-berries, and the commonest
      weeds by the road,
And the old drunkard staggering home from the outhouse
      of the tavern whence he had lately risen,
And the schoolmistress that pass'd, on her way to the school,
And the friendly boys that pass'd, and the quarrelsome
      boys,
And the tidy and fresh-cheek'd girls, and the barefoot
      negro boy and girl,
And all the changes of city and country wherever he went.

His own parents, he that had father'd him and she that had
      conceiv'd him in her womb and birth'd him,
They gave this child more of themselves than that,
They gave him afterward every day, they became part of
      him.

The mother at home quietly placing the dishes on the
      supper-table,
The mother with mild words, clean her cap and gown, a
      wholesome odor falling off her person and clothes as
      she walks by,
The father, strong, self-sufficient, manly, mean, anger'd,
      unjust,
The blow, the quick loud word, the tight bargain, the
      crafty lure,
The family usages, the language, the company, the furni-
      ture, the yearning and swelling heart,
Affection that will not be gainsay'd, the sense of what is
      real, the thought if after all it should prove unreal,
The doubts of day-time and the doubts of night-time, the
      curious whether and how,
Whether that which appears so is so, or is it all flashes and
      specks?

Men and women crowding fast in the streets, if they are
    not flashes and specks what are they?
The streets themselves and the facades of houses, and goods
    in the windows,
Vehicles, teams, the heavy-plank'd wharves, the huge cross-
    ing at the ferries,
The village on the highland seen from afar at sunset, the
    river between,
Shadows, aureola and mist, the light falling on roofs and
    gables of white or brown two miles off,
The schooner near by sleepily dropping down the tide, the
    little boat slack-tow'd astern,
The hurrying tumbling waves, quick-broken crests, slap-
    ping,
The stratas of color'd clouds, the long bar of maroon-tint
    away solitary by itself, the spread of purity it lies
    motionless in,
The horizon's edge, the flying sea-crow , the fragrance of
    salt marsh and shore mud,
These became part of that child who went forth every day,
    and who now goes, and will always go forth every
    day.

O Captain! My Captain! [1865]

O Captain! my Captain! our fearful trip is done,
The ship has weather'd every rack, the prize we sought is
            won,
The port is near, the bells I hear, the people all exulting,
While follow eyes the steady keel, the vessel grim and
            daring;
      But O heart! heart! heart!
        O the bleeding drops of red,
            Where on the deck my Captain lies,
              Fallen cold and dead.

O Captain! my Captain! rise up and hear the bells;
Rise up—for you the flag is flung—for you the bugle trills,
For you bouquets and ribbon'd wreaths—for you the
            shores a-crowding,
For you they call, the swaying mass, their eager faces
            turning;
      Here Captain! dear father!
        The arm beneath your head!
            It is some dream that on the deck,
              You've fallen cold and dead.

My Captain does not answer, his lips are pale and still,
My father does not feel my arm, he has no pulse nor will,
The ship is anchor'd safe and sound, its voyage closed and
            done,
From fearful trip the victor ship comes in with object won;
      Exult O shores, and ring O bells!
        But I with mournful tread,
            Walk the deck my Captain lies,
              Fallen cold and dead.

Beat! Beat! Drums! [1865]
From "Drum-Taps"

Beat! beat! drums—blow! bugles, blow!
Through the windows—through doors—burst like a
        ruthless force,
Into the solemn church, and scatter the congregation,
Into the school where the scholar is studying;
Leave not the bridegroom quiet—no happiness must he
        have now with his bride,
Nor the peaceful farmer any peace, ploughing his field or
        gathering his grain,
So fierce you whirr and pound you drums—so shrill you
        bugles blow.

Beat! beat! drums—blow! bugles! blow!
Over the traffic of cities—over the rumble of wheels in the
        streets;
Are beds prepared for sleepers at night in the houses? no
        sleepers must sleep in those beds.
No bargainers' bargains by day—no brokers or speculators
        —would they continue?
Would the talkers be talking? would the singer attempt to
        sing?
Would the lawyer rise in the court to state his case before
        the judge?
Then rattle quicker, heavier drums—you bugles wilder
        blow.

Beat! beat! drums!—blow! bugles! blow!
Make no parley— stop for no expostulation,
Mind not the timid—mind not the weeper or prayer,
Mind not the old man beseeching the young man,
Let not the child's voice be heard, nor the mother's
        entreaties,

Make even the trestles to shake the dead where they lie
        awaiting the hearses,
So strong you thump O terrible drums—so loud you
bugles blow.

A Hand-Mirror

Hold it up sternly—see this it sends back, (who is
    it? is it you?)
Outside fair costume, within ashes and filth,
No more a flashing eye, no more a sonorous voice or springy
    step,
Now some slave's eye, voice, hands, step,
A drunkard's breath, unwholesome eater's face, venerealee's
    flesh,
Lungs rotting away piecemeal, stomach sour and cankerous,
Joints rheumatic, bowels clogged with abomination,
Blood circulating dark and poisonous streams,
Words babble, hearing and touch callous,
No brain, no heart left, no magnetism of sex;
Such from one look in this looking-glass ere you go hence,
Such a result so soon—and from such a beginning!

Cavalry Crossing a Ford

A line in long array where they wind betwixt green
    islands,
They take a serpentine course, their arms flash in the sun—
    hark to the musical clank,
Behold the silvery river, in it the splashing horses loiter-
    ing stop to drink,
Behold the brown-faced men, each group, each person a
    picture, the negligent rest on the saddles,
Some emerge on the opposite bank, others are just entering
    the ford—while,
Scarlet and blue and snowy white,
The guidon flags flutter gayly in the wind.

When I Heard at the Close
of the Day

When I heard at the close of the day how my name
      had been receiv'd with plaudits in the capitol, still it
      was not a happy night for me that follow'd,
And else when I carous'd, or when my plans were accom-
      plish'd, still I was not happy,
But the day when I rose at dawn from the bed of perfect
      health, refresh'd, singing, inhaling the ripe breath of
      autumn,
When I saw the full moon in the west grow pale and dis-
      appear in the morning light,
When I wander'd alone over the beach, and undressing
      bathed, laughing with the cool waters, and saw the
      sun rise,
And when I thought how my dear friend my lover was on
      his way coming, O then I was happy,
O then each breath tasted sweeter, and all that day my food
      nourish'd me more, and the beautiful day pass'd well,
And the next came with equal joy, and with the next at
      evening came my friend,
And that night while all was still I heard the waters roll
      slowly continually up the shores,
I heard the hissing rustle of the liquid and sands as
      directed to me whispering to congratulate me,
For the one I love most lay sleeping by me under the same
      cover in the cool night,
In the stillness in the autumn moonbeams his face was in-
      clined toward me,
And his arm lay lightly around my breast—and that night
      I was happy.

A Noiseless Patient Spider [1871]

A noiseless patient spider,
I mark'd where on a little promontory it stood isolated,
Mark'd how to explore the vacant vast surrounding,
It launch'd forth filament, filament, filament, out of itself,
Ever unreeling them, ever tirelessly speeding them.

And you O my soul where you stand,
Surrounded, detached, in measureless oceans of space,
Ceaselessly musing, venturing, throwing, seeking the
          spheres to connect them,

Till the bridge you will need be form'd, till the ductile
          anchor hold,
Till the gossamer thread you fling catch somewhere, O my
          soul.

Out of the Cradle Endlessly Rocking [1860]

Out of the cradle endlessly rocking,
Out of the mocking-bird's throat, the musical shuttle,
Out of the Ninth-month midnight,
Over the sterile sands and the fields beyond, where the
          child leaving his bed wander'd alone, bareheaded,
          barefoot,
Down from the shower'd halo,
Up from the mystic play of shadows twining and twisting
          as if they were alive,
Out from the patches of briers and blackberries,
From the memories of the bird that chanted to me,
From your memories sad brother, from the fitful risings
          and fallings I heard,
From under that yellow half-moon late-risen and swollen
          as if with tears,
From those beginning notes of yearning and love there in
          the mist,

From the thousand responses of my heart never to cease,
From the myriad thence-arous'd words,
From the word stronger and more delicious than any,
From such as now they start the scene revisiting,
As a flock, twittering, rising, or overhead passing,
Borne hither, ere all eludes me, hurriedly,
A man, yet by these tears a little boy again,
Throwing myself on the sand, confronting the waves,
I, chanter of pains and joys, uniter of here and hereafter,
Taking all hints to use them, but swiftly leaping beyond
        them,
A reminiscence sing.

Once Paumanok,
When the lilac-scent was in the air and Fifth-month grass
        was growing,
Up this seashore in some briers,
Two feather'd guests from Alabama, two together,
And their nest, and four light-green eggs spotted with
        brown,
And every day the he-bird to and fro near at hand,
And every day the she-bird crouch'd on her nest, silent,
        with bright eyes,
And every day I, a curious boy, never too close, never
        disturbing them,
Cautiously peering, absorbing, translating.

Shine! shine! shine!
Pour down your warmth, great sun!
While we bask, we two together.

Two together!
Winds blow south, or winds blow north,
Day come white, or night come black,
Home, or rivers and mountains from home,
Singing all time, minding no time,
While we two keep together.

Till of a sudden,

May-be kill'd, unknown to her mate,
One forenoon the she-bird crouch'd not on the nest,
Nor return'd that afternoon, nor the next,
Nor ever appear'd again.

And thenceforward all summer in the sound of the sea,
And at night under the full of the moon in calmer weather,
Over the hoarse surging of the sea,
Or flitting from brier to brier by day,
I saw, I heard at intervals the remaining one, the he-bird,
The solitary guest from Alabama.

Blow! blow! blow!
Blow up sea-winds along Paumanok's shore;
I wait and I wait till you blow my mate to me.

Yes, when the stars glisten'd,
All night long on the prong of a moss-scallop'd stake,
Down almost amid the slapping waves,
Sat the lone singer wonderful causing tears.

He call'd on his mate,
He pour'd forth the meanings which I of all men know.

Yes my brother I know,
The rest might not, but I have treasur'd every note,
For more than once dimly down to the beach gliding,
Silent, avoiding the moonbeams, blending myself with the
          shadows,
Recalling now the obscure shapes, the echoes, the sounds
          and sights after their sorts,
The white arms out in the breakers tirelessly tossing,
I, with bare feet, a child, the wind wafting my hair,
Listen'd long and long.

Listen'd to keep, to sing, now translating the notes,
Following you my brother.

Soothe! soothe! soothe!

Close on its wave soothes the wave behind,
And again another behind embracing and lapping, every one close,
But my love soothes not me, not me.

Low hangs the moon, it rose late,
It is lagging—O I think it is heavy with love, with love.

O madly the sea pushes upon the land,
With love, with love.

O night! do I not see my love fluttering out among the breakers?
What is that little black thing I see there in the white?

Loud! loud! loud!
Loud I call to you, my love!
High and clear I shoot my voice over the waves,
Surely you must know who is here, is here,
You must know who I am, my love.

Low-hanging moon!
What is that dusky spot in your brown yellow?
O it is the shape, the shape of my mate!
O moon do not keep her from me any longer.

Land! land! O land!
Whichever way I turn, O I think you could give me my mate back
        again if you only would,
For I am almost sure I see her dimly whichever way I look.

O rising stars!
Perhaps the one I want so much will rise, will rise with some of
        you.

O throat! O trembling throat!
Sound clearer through the atmosphere!
Pierce the woods, the earth,
Somewhere listening to catch you must be the one I want.

Shake out carols!

Solitary here, the night's carols!
Carols of lonesome love! death's carols!
Carols under that lagging, yellow, waning moon!
O under the moon where she droops almost down into the sea!
O reckless despairing carols.

But soft! sink low!
Soft! let me just murmur,
And do you wait a moment you husky-nois'd sea,
For somewhere I believe I heard my mate responding to me,
So faint, I must be still, be still to listen,
But not altogether still, for then she might not come immediately
        to me.

Hither my love!
Here I am! here!
With this just-sustain'd note I announce myself to you,
This gentle call is for you my love, for you.

Do not be decoy'd elsewhere,
That is the whistle of the wind, it is not my voice,
That is the fluttering, the fluttering of the spray,
Those are the shadows of leaves.

O darkness! O in vain!
O I am very sick and sorrowful.

O brown halo in the sky near the moon, drooping upon the sea!
O troubled reflection in the sea!
O throat! O throbbing heart!
And I singing uselessly, uselessly all the night.

O past! O happy life! O songs of joy!
In the air, in the woods, over fields,
Loved! loved! loved! loved! loved!
But my mate no more, no more with me!
We two together no more.

The aria sinking,

All else continuing, the stars shining,
The winds blowing, the notes of the bird continuous
    echoing,
With angry moans the fierce old mother incessantly
    moaning,
On the sands of Paumanok's shore gray and rustling,
The yellow half moon enlarged, sagging down, drooping,
    the face of the sea almost touching,

The boy ecstatic, with his bare feet the waves, with his hair
    the atmosphere dallying,
The love in the heart long pent, now loose, now at last
    tumultuously bursting,
The aria's meaning, the ears, the soul, swiftly depositing,
The strange tears down the checks coursing,
The colloquy there, the trio, each uttering,
The undertone, the savage old mother incessantly crying,
To the boy's soul's questions suddenly timing, some
    drown'd secret hissing,
To the outsetting bard.

Demon or bird! (said the boy's soul,)
Is it indeed toward your mate you sing? or is it really to
    me?
For I, that was a child, my tongue's use sleeping, now I
    have heard you,
Now in a moment I know what I am for, I awake,
And already a thousand singers, a thousand songs, clearer,
    louder and more sorrowful than yours,
A thousand warbling echoes have started to life within me,
    never to die.

O you singer solitary, singing by yourself, projecting me,
O solitary me listening, never more shall I cease
    perpetuating you,
Never more shall I escape, never more the reverberations.
Never more the cries of unsatisfied love be absent from
    me,
Never again leave me to be the peaceful child I was before

what there in the night,
By the sea under the yellow and sagging moon,
The messenger there arous'd, the fire, the sweet hell
        within,
The unknown want, the destiny of me.

O give me the clew! (it lurks in the night here somewhere,)
O if I am to have so much, let me have more!

A word then, (for I will conquer it,)
The word final, superior to all,

Subtle, sent up—what is it?—I listen:
Are you whispering it, and have been all the time, you sea
        waves?
Is that it from your liquid rims and wet sands?

Whereto answering, the sea,
Delaying not, hurrying not,
Whisper'd me through the night, and very plainly before
        daybreak,
Lisp'd to me the low and delicious word death,
And again death, death, death, death,
Hissing melodious, neither like the bird nor like my
        arous'd child's heart,
But edging near as privately for me rustling at my feet,
Creeping thence steadily up to my ears and laving me
        softly all over,
Death, death, death, death, death.

Which I do not forget,
But fuse the song of my dusky demon and brother,
That he sang to me in the moonlight on Paumanok's
        gray beach,
With the thousand responsive songs at random,
My own songs awaked from that hour,
And with them the key, the word up from the waves,
The word of the sweetest song and all songs,

That strong and delicious word which, creeping to my
        feet,
(Or like some old crone rocking the cradle, swathed in
        sweet garments, bending aside.)
The sea whisper'd me.

Crossing Brooklyn Ferry [1836]

1

Flood-tide below me! I see you face to face!
Clouds of the west—sun there half an hour high— I see you
        also face to face.

Crowds of men and women attired in the usual costumes,
        how curious you are to me!
On the ferry-boats the hundreds and hundreds that cross
        returning home, are more curious to me than you
        suppose,
And you that shall cross from shore to shore years hence
        are more to me, and more in my meditations, than you
might suppose.

2

The impalpable sustenance of me from all things at all hours
        of the day,
The simple, compact, well-join'd scheme, myself
        disintegrated, every one disintegrated yet part of the
        scheme,
The similitudes of the past and those of the future,
The glories strung like beads on my smallest sights and
        hearings, on the walk in the street and the passage over
        the river,
The current rushing so swiftly and swimming with me far
        away,

The others that are to follow me, the ties between me and
    them,
The certainty of others, the life, love, sight, hearing of
    others.

Others will enter the gates of the ferry and cross from
    shore to shore,
Others will watch the run of the flood-tide,
Others will see the shipping of Manhattan north and west,
    and the heights of Brooklyn to the south and east,
Others will see the islands large and small;
Fifty years hence, others will see them as they cross, the
    sun half an hour high,
A hundred years hence, or ever so many hundred years
    hence, others will see them,
Will enjoy the sunset, the pouring-in of the flood-tide, the
    falling-back to the sea of the ebb-tide.

3

It avails not, time nor place—distance avails not,
I am with you, you men and women of a generation, or
    ever so many generations hence,
Just as you feel when you look on the river and sky, so I
    felt,
Just as any of you is one of a living crowd, I was one of a
    crowd,
Just as you are refresh'd by the gladness of the river and
    the bright flow, I was refresh'd,
Just as you stand and lean on the rail, yet hurry with the
    swift current, I stood yet was hurried,
Just as you look on the numberless masts of ships and the
    thick-stemm'd pipes of steamboats, I look'd.

I too many and many a time cross'd the river of old,
Watched the Twelfth-month sea-gulls, saw them high in
    the air floating with the motionless wings, oscillating their
    bodies,
Saw how the glistening yellow lit up parts of their bodies

and left the rest in strong shadow,
Saw the slow-wheeling circles and the gradual edging
    toward the south,
Saw the reflection of the summer sky in the water,
Had my eyes dazzled by the shimmering track of beams,
Look'd at the fine centrifugal spokes of light round the
    shape of my head in the sunlit water,
Look'd on the haze on the hills southward and south-
    westward,
Look'd on the vapor as it flew in fleeces tinged with
    violet,
Look'd toward the lower bay to notice the vessels arriving,
Saw their approach, saw aboard those that were near me,
Saw the white sails of schooners and sloops, saw the ships
    at anchor,
The sailors at work in the rigging or out astride the spars,
The round masts, the swinging motion of the hulls, the
    slender serpentine pennants,
The large and small steamers in motion, the pilots in their
    pilot-houses,
The white wake left by the passage, the quick tremulous
    whirl of the wheels,
The flags of all nations, the falling of them at sunset,
The scallop-edged waves in the twilight, the ladled cups,
    the frolicsome crests and glistening,
The stretch afar growing dimmer and dimmer, the gray
    walls of the granite storehouses by the docks,
On the river the shadowy group, the big steam-tug closely
    flank'd on each side by the barges, the hay-boat, the
    belated lighter,
On the neighboring shore the fires from the foundry
    chimneys burning high and glaringly into the night,
Casting their flicker of black contrasted with wild red and
    yellow light over the tops of houses, and down into
    the clefts of streets.

4

These and all else were to me the same as they are to you,

I loved well those cities, loved well the stately and rapid
    river,
The men and women I saw were all near to me,
Others the same—others who look back on me because I
    look'd forward to them,
(The time will come, though I stop here to-day and
    to-night.)

5

What is it then between us?
What is the count of the scores or hundreds of years
between us?

Whatever it is, it avails not—distance avails not, and place
    avails not,
I too lived, Brooklyn of ample hills was mine,
I too walk'd the streets of Manhattan island, and bathed
    in the waters around it,
I too felt the curious abrupt questionings stir within me,
In the day among crowds of people sometimes they came
    upon me,
In my walks home late at night or as I lay in my bed they
    came upon me,
I too had been struck from the float forever held in
    solution,
I too had receiv'd identity by my body,
That I was I knew was of my body, and what I should be I
    knew I should be of my body.

6

It is not upon you alone the dark patches fall,
The dark threw its patches down upon me also,
The best I had done seem'd to me blank and suspicious,
My great thoughts as I supposed them, were they not in
    reality meagre?
Nor is it you alone who know what it is to be evil,
I am he who knew what it was to be evil,

I too knitted the old knot of contrariety,
Blabb'd, blush'd, resented, lied, stole, grudg'd,
Had guile, anger, lust, hot wishes I dared not speak,
Was wayward, vain, greedy, shallow, sly, cowardly,
    malignant,
The wolf, the snake, the hog, not wanting in me,
The cheating look, the frivolous word, the adulterous wish,
    not wanting,
Refusals, hates, postponements, meanness, laziness, none of
    these wanting,
Was one with the rest, the days and haps of the rest,
Was call'd by my nighest name by clear loud voices of
    young men as they saw me approaching or passing,
Felt their arms on my neck as I stood, or the negligent
    leaning of their flesh against me as I sat,
Saw many I loved in the street or ferry-boat or public
    assembly, yet never told them a word,
Lived the same life with the rest, the same old laughing,
    gnawing, sleeping,
Play'd the part that still looks back on the actor or actress,
The same old role, the role that is what we make it, as
    great as we like,
Or as small as we like, or both great and small.

7

Closer yet I approach you,
What thought you have of me now, I had as much of you
    —I laid in my stores in advance,
I consider'd long and seriously of you before you were born.

Who was to know what should come home to me?
Who knows but I am enjoying this?
Who knows, for all the distance, but I am as good as
    looking at you now, for all you cannot see me?

8

Ah, what can ever be more stately and admirable to me

than mast-hemm'd Manhattan?
River and sunset and scallop-edg'd waves of flood-tide?
The sea-gulls oscillating their bodies, the hay-boat in the
    twilight, and the belated lighter?
What gods can exceed these that clasp me by the hand, and
    with voices I love call me promptly and loudly by my
    nighest name as I approach?

What is more subtle than this which ties me to the woman
    or man that looks in my face?
Which fuses me into you now, and pours my meaning into
    you?

We understand then do we not?
What I promis'd without mentioning it, have you not
    accepted?
What the study could not teach—what the preaching could
    not accomplish is accomplish'd, is it not?

9

Flow on, river! flow with the flood-tide, and ebb with the
    ebb-tide!
Frolic on, crested and scallop-edg'd waves!
Gorgeous clouds of the sunset! drench with your splendor
    me, or the men and women generations after me!
Cross from shore to shore, countless crowds of passengers!
Stand up, tall masts of Mannahatta! stand up, beautiful hills
    of Brooklyn!
Throb! baffled and curious brain! throw out questions and
    answers!
Suspend here and everywhere, eternal float of solution!
Gaze, loving and thirsting eyes, in the house or street or
    public assembly!
Sound out, voices of young men! loudly and musically call
    me by my nighest name!
Live, old life! play the part that looks back on the actor or
    actress!
Play the old role, the role that is great or small according

as one makes it!
Consider, you who peruse me, whether I may not in
     unknown ways be looking upon you;
Be firm, rail over the river, to support those who lean
     idly, yet haste with the hasting current;
Fly on, sea-birds! fly sideways, or wheel in large circles
     high in the air;
Receive the summer sky, you water, and faithfully hold it
     till all downcast eyes have time to take it from you!
Diverge, fine spokes of light, from the shape of my head,
     or any one's head, in the sunlit water!
Come on, ships from the lower bay! pass up or down,
     white-sail'd schooners, sloops, lighters!
Flaunt away, flags of all nations! be duly lower'd at sunset!
Burn high your fires, foundry chimneys! cast black shadows
     at nightfall! cast red and yellow light over the tops of
     the houses!
Appearances, now or henceforth, indicate what you are,
You necessary film, continue to envelop the soul,
About my body for me, and your body for you, be hung
     our divinest aromas,
Thrive, cities—bring your freight, bring your shows, ample
     and sufficient rivers,
Expand, being than which none else is perhaps more spiritual,
Keep your places, objects than which none else is more lasting.

You have waited, you always wait, you dumb, beautiful ministers,
We receive you with free sense at last, and are insatiate henceforward,
Not you any more shall be able to foil us, or withhold yourselves from
     us,
We use you, and do not cast you aside—we plant you permanently
within us,
We fathom you not—we love you—there is perfection in you also,
You furnish your parts toward eternity,
Great or small, you furnish your parts toward the soul.

Song of Myself [1855]

I

I celebrate myself, and sing myself,
And what I assume you shall assume.
For every atom belonging to me as good belongs to you.

I loafe and invite my soul,
I lean and loafe at my ease observing a spear of summer grass.

My tongue, every atom of my blood, form'd from this soil, this
          air,
Born here of parents born here from parents the same, and
              their parents the same,
I now thirty-seven years old in perfect health begin,
Hoping to cease not till death.

Creeds and schools in abeyance,
Retiring back a while sufficed at what they are, but never
              forgotten,
I harbor for good or bad, I permit to speak at every hazard,
Nature without check with original energy.

2

Houses and rooms are full of perfumes, the shelves are crowded
          with perfumes,
I breathe the fragrance myself and know it and like it,
The distillation would intoxicate me also, but I shall not let it.
The atmosphere is not a perfume, it has no taste of the
          distillation, it is odorless,
It is for my mouth forever, I am in love with it,
I will go to the bank by the wood and become undisguised and
          naked,
I am mad for it to be in contact with me.

The smoke of my own breath,

Echoes, ripples, buzz'd whispers, love-root, silk-thread, crotch
    and vine,
My respiration and inspiration, the beating of my heart, the
    passing of blood and air through my lungs,
The sniff of green leaves and dry leaves, and of the shore and
    dark-color'd sea-rocks, and of hay in the barn,
The sound of the belch'd words of my voice loos'd to the eddies
    of the wind,
A few light kisses, a few embraces, a reaching around of arms,
The play of shine and shade on the trees as the supple boughs
    wag,
The delight alone or in the rush of the streets, or along the
    fields and hill-sides,
The feeling of health, the full-moon trill, the song of me rising
    from bed and meeting the sun.

Have you reckon'd a thousand acres much? have you reckon'd
    the earth much?
Have you practis'd so long to learn to read?
Have you felt so proud to get at the meaning of poems?

Stop this day and night with me and you shall possess the origin
    of all poems,
You shall possess the good of the earth and sun, (there are
    millions of suns left,)
You shall no longer take things at second or third hand, nor
    look through the eyes of the dead, nor feed on the
    spectres in books,
You shall not look through my eyes either, nor take things
    from me,
You shall listen to all sides and filter them from your self.

3

I have heard what the talkers were talking, the talk of the
    beginning and the end,
But I do not talk of the beginning or the end.

There was never any more inception than there is now,

Nor any more youth or age than there is now,
And will never be any more perfection than there is now,
Nor any more heaven than there is now.

Urge and urge and urge,
Always the procreant urge of the world.
Out of the dimness opposite equals advance, always substance
        and increase, always sex,
Always a knit of identity, always distinction, always a breed of
        life.

To elaborate is no avail, learn'd and unlearn'd feel that it is so.

Sure as the most certain sure, plumb in the uprights, well
        entretied, braced in the beams.
Stout as a horse, affectionate, haughty, electrical,
I and this mystery here we stand.

Clear and sweet is my soul, and clear and sweet is all that is not
        my soul.

Lack one lacks both, and the unseen is proved by the seen,
Till that becomes unseen and receives proof in its turn.

Showing the best and dividing it from the worst age vexes age,
Knowing the perfect fitness and equanimity of things, while
        they discuss I am silent, and go bathe and admire myself.
Welcome is every organ and attribute of me, and of any man
        hearty and clean,
Not an inch nor a particle of an inch is vile, and none shall be
        less familiar than the rest.

I am satisfied—I see, dance, laugh, sing;
As the hugging and loving bed-fellow sleeps at my side
        through the night, and withdraws at the peep of the day
        with stealthy tread,
Leaving me baskets cover'd with white towels swelling the house
        with their plenty,

Shall I postpone my acceptation and realization and scream at
          my eyes,
That they turn from gazing after and down the road,
And forthwith cipher and show me to a cent,
Exactly the value of one and exactly the value of two, and which
          is ahead?

Trippers and askers surround me,
People I meet, the effect upon me of my early life or the ward
          and city I live in, or the nation,
The latest dates, discoveries, inventions, societies, authors old
          and new,
My dinner, dress, associates, looks, compliments, dues,
The real or fancied indifference of some man or woman I love,
The sickness of one of my folks or of myself, or ill-doing or
          loss or lack of money, or depressions or exaltations,
Battles, the horrors of fratricidal war, the fever of doubtful
          news, the fitful events;
These come to me days and nights and go from me again,
But they are not the Me myself.

Apart from the pulling and hauling stands what I am,
Stands amused, complacent, compassionating, idle, unitary,
Looks down, is erect, or bends an arm on an impalpable certain
          rest,
Looking with side-curved head curious what will come next,
Both in and out of the game and watching and wondering at it.

Backward I see in my own days where I sweated through fog
          with linguists and contenders,
I have no mockings or arguments, I witness and wait.

5

I believe in you my soul, the other I am must not abase itself to
          you,
And you must not be abased to the other.

Loaf with me on the grass, loose the stop from your throat,

Not words, not music or rhyme I want, not custom or lecture,
        not even the best,
Only the lull I like, the hum of your valvèd voice.
I mind how once we lay such a transparent summer morning,
How you settled your head athwart my hips and gently turn'd
        over upon me,
And parted the shirt from my bosom-bone, and plunged your
        tongue to my bare-stript heart,
And reach'd till you felt my beard, and reach'd till you held my
        feet.

Swiftly arose and spread around me the peace and knowledge
        that pass all the argument of the earth,
And I know that the hand of God is the promise of my own,
And I know that the spirit of God is the brother of my own,
And that all the men ever born are also my brothers, and the
        women my sisters and lovers,
And that a kelson of the creation is love,
And limitless are leaves stiff or dropping in the fields,
And brown ants in the little wells beneath them,
And mossy scabs of the worm fence, heap'd stones, elder, mul-
        lein and poke-weed.

6

A child said *What is the grass?* fetching it to me with full hands,
How could I answer the child? I do not know what it is any more
        than he.

I guess it must be the flag of my disposition, out of hopeful
        green stuff woven.

Or I guess it is the handkerchief of the Lord,
A scented gift and remembrancer designedly dropt,
Bearing the owner's name someway in the corners, that we may
        see and remark, and say *Whose?*

Or I guess the grass is itself a child, the produced babe of the
        vegetation.

Or I guess it is a uniform hieroglyphic,
And it means, Sprouting alike in broad zones and narrow zones,
Growing among black folks as among white,
Kanuck, Tuckahoe, Congressman, Cuff, I give them the same, I
    receive them the same.

And now it seems to me the beautiful uncut hair of graves.

Tenderly will I use you curling grass,
It may be you transpire from the breasts of young men,
It may be if I had known them I would have loved them,
It may be you are from old people, or from offspring taken
    soon out of their mothers' laps.
And here you are the mothers' laps.
This grass is very dark to be from the white heads of old moth-
    ers,
Darker than the colorless beards of old men,
Dark to come from under the faint red roofs of mouths.

O I perceive after all so many uttering tongues,
And I perceive they do not come from the roofs of mouths for
    nothing.

I wish I could translate the hints about the dead young men and
    women,
And the hints about old men and mothers, and the offspring
    taken soon out of their laps.

What do you think has become of the young and old men?
And what do you think has become of the women and children?

They are alive and well somewhere,
The smallest sprout shows there is really no death,
And if ever there was it led forward life, and does not wait at the
    end to arrest it,
And ceas'd the moment life appear'd.

All goes onward and outward, nothing collapses,
And to die is different from what any one supposed, and luckier.

7

Has any one supposed it lucky to be born?
I hasten to inform him or her it is just as lucky to die, and I
    know it.

I pass death with the dying and birth with the new-wash'd
            babe, and am not contain'd between my hat and boots,
And peruse manifold objects, no two alike and every one good,
The earth good and the stars good, and their adjuncts all good.

I am not an earth nor an adjunct of an earth,
I am the mate and companion of people, all just as immortal and
            fathomless as myself,
(They do not know how immortal, but I know.)

Every kind for itself and its own, for me mine male and female,
For me those that have been boys and that love women,
For me the man that is proud and feels how it stings to be
    slighted,
For me the sweet-heart and the old maid, for me mothers and
    the mothers of mothers,
For me lips that have smiled, eyes that have shed tears,
For me children and the begetters of children.

Undrape! you are not guilty to me, nor stale nor discarded,
I see through the broadcloth and gingham whether or no,
And am around, tenacious, acquisitive, tireless, and cannot be
    shaken away.

8

The little one sleeps in its cradle,
I lift the gauze and look a long time, and silently brush away
    flies with my hand.

The youngster and the red-faced girl turn aside up the bushy
    hill,
I peeringly view them from the top.

The suicide sprawls on the bloody floor of the bedroom,
I witness the corpse with its dabbled hair, I note where the
        pistol has fallen.

The blab of the pave, tires of carts, sluff of boot-soles, talk of the
        promenaders,
The heavy omnibus, the driver with his interrogating thumb,
        the clank of the shod horses on the granite floor,
The snow-sleighs, clinking, shouted jokes, pelts of snow-balls,
The hurrahs for popular favorites, the fury of rous'd mobs,
The flap of the curtain'd litter, a sick man inside borne to the
        hospital,
The meeting of enemies, the sudden oath, the blows and fall,
The exciting crowd, the policeman with his star quickly working
        his passage to the centre of the crowd,
The impassive stones that receive and return so many echoes,
What groans of over-fed or half-starv'd who fall sunstruck or in
        fits,
What exclamations of women taken suddenly who hurry home
        and give birth to babes,
What living and buried speech is always vibrating here, what
        howls restrain'd by decorum,
Arrests of criminals, slights, adulterous offers made,
        acceptances, rejections with convex lips,
I mind them or the show or resonance of them—I come and I
        depart.

9

The big doors of the country barn stand open and ready,
The dried grass of the harvest-time loads the slow-drawn wagon,
The clear light plays on the brown gray and green intertinged,
The armfuls are pack'd to the sagging mow.

I am there, I help, I came stretch'd atop of the load,
I felt its soft jolts, one leg reclined on the other,
I jumped from the cross-beams and seize the clover and timothy,
And roll head over heels and tangle my hair full of wisps.

10

Alone far in the wilds and mountains I hunt,
Wandering amazed at my own lightness and glee,
In the late afternoon choosing a safe spot to pass the night,
Kindling a fire and broiling the fresh-kill'd game,
Falling asleep on the gather'd leaves with my dog and gun by
    my side.
The Yankee clipper is under her sky-sails, she cuts the sparkle
        and scud,
My eyes settle the land, I bend at her prow or shout joyously
        from the deck.

The boatmen and clam-diggers arose early and stopt for me,
I tuck'd my trowser-ends in my boots and went and had a good
        time;
You should have been with us that day round the
        chowder-kettle.

I saw the marriage of the trapper in the open air in the far west,
        the bride was a red girl,
Her father and his friends sat near cross-legged and dumbly
        smoking, they had moccasins to their feet and large
        thick blankets hanging from their shoulders,
On a bank lounged the trapper, he was drest mostly in skins,
        his luxuriant beard and curls protected his neck, he held
        his bride by the hand,
She had long eyelashes, her head was bare, her coarse straight
        locks descended upon her voluptuous limbs and reach'd
        to her feet.

The runaway slave came to my house and stopt outside,
I heard his motions crackling the twigs of the woodpile,
Through the swung half-door of the kitchen I saw him, limpsy
        and weak,
And went where he sat on a log and led him in and assured him,
And brought water and fill'd a tub for his sweated body and
        bruis'd his feet,
And gave him a room that enter'd from my own, and gave him

some coarse clean clothes,
And remember perfectly well his revolving eyes and his
    awkwardness,
And remember putting plasters on the galls of his neck and
    ankles;
He staid with me a week before he was recuperated and pass'd
    north,
I had him sit next me at table, my fire-lock lean'd in the corner.

11

Twenty-eight young men bathe by the shore,
Twenty-eight young men and all so friendly;
Twenty-eight years of womanly life and all so lonesome.

She owns the fine house by the rise of the bank,
She hides handsome and richly drest aft the blinds of the
    window.

Which of the young men does she like the best?
Ah the homeliest of them is beautiful to her.

Where are you off to, lady? for I see you,
You splash in the water there, yet stay stock still in your room.

Dancing and laughing along the beach came the twenty-ninth
    bather,
The rest did not see her, but she saw them and loved them.

The beards of the young men glisten'd with wet, it ran from
    their long hair,
Little streams pass'd all over their bodies.

An unseen hand also pass'd over their bodies,
It descended tremblingly from their temples and ribs.

The young men float on their backs, their white bellies bulge to
    the sun, they do not ask who seizes fast to them,
They do not know who puffs and declines with pendant and

bending arch,
They do not think whom they souse with spray.

12

The butcher-boy puts off his killing-clothes, or sharpens his
        knife at the stall in the market,
I loiter enjoying his repartee and his shuffle and break-down.

Blacksmiths with grimed and hairy chests environ the anvil,
Each has main-sledge, they are all out, there is a great heat in
        the fire.

From the cinder-strew'd threshold I follow their movements,
The lithe sheer of their waists plays even with their massive
        arms,
Overhand the hammers swing, overhand so slow, overhand so
        sure,
They do not hasten, each man hits in his place.

13

The negro holds firmly the reins of his four horses, the block
        swags underneath on its tied-over chain,
The negro that drives the long dray of the stone-yard, steady
        and tall he stands pois'd on one leg on the string-piece,
His blue shirt exposes his ample neck and breast and loosens
        over his hip-band,
His glance is calm and commanding, he tosses the slouch of his
        hat away from his forehead,
The sun falls on his crispy hair and mustache, falls on the black
        of his polish'd and perfect limbs.

I behold the picturesque giant and love him, and I do not stop
        there, I go with the team also.

In me the caresser of life wherever moving, backward as well as
        forward sluing,

To niches aside and junior bending, not a person or object
        missing,
Absorbing all to myself and for this song.
Oxen that rattle the yoke and chain or halt in the leafy shade,
        what is that you express in your eyes?
It seems to me more than all the print I have read in my life.

My tread scares the wood-drake and wood-duck on my distant
        and day-long ramble,
They rise together, they slowly circle around.

I believe in those wing'd purposes,
And acknowledge red, yellow, white, playing within me,
And consider green and violet and the tufted crown intentional,
And do not call the tortoise unworthy because she is not
        something else,
And the jay in the woods never studied the gamut, yet trills
        pretty well to me,
And the look of the bay mare shames silliness out of me.

14

The wild gander leads his flock through the cool night,
Ya-honk he says, and sounds it down to me like an invitation,
The pert you suppose it meaningless, but I listening close,
Find its purpose and place up there toward the wintry sky.

The sharp-hoof'd moose of the north, the cat on the house-sill,
        the chickadee, the prairie-dog,
The litter of the grunting sow as they tug at her teats,
The brood of the turkey-hens and she with her half-spread
        wings,
I see in them and myself the same old law.

The press of my foot to the earth springs a hundred affections,
They scorn the best I can do to relate them.

I am enamour'd of growing out-doors,
Of men that live among cattle or taste of the ocean or woods,

Of the builders and steerers of ships and the wielders of axes
          and mauls, and the drivers of horses,
I can eat and sleep with them week in and week out.

What is commonest, cheapest, nearest, easiest, is Me,
Me going in for my chances, spending for vast returns,
Adorning myself to bestow myself on the first that will take me,
Not asking the sky to come down to my good will,
Scattering it freely forever.

15

The pure contralto sings in the organ loft,
The carpenter dresses his plank, the tongue of his foreplane
          whistles its wild ascending lisp,
The married and unmarried children ride home to their
          Thanksgiving dinner,
The pilot seizes the king-pin, he heaves down with a strong arm,
The mate stands braced in the whale-boat, lance and harpoon
          are ready,
The duck-shooter walks by silent and cautious stretches,
The deacons are ordain'd with cross'd hands at the altar,
The spinning-girl retreats and advances to the hum of the big
          wheel,
The farmer stops by the bars as he walks on a First-day loafe
          and looks at the oats and rye,
The lunatic is carried at last to the asylum a confirm'd case,
(He will never sleep any more as he did in the cot in his mother's
          bedroom;)
The jour printer with gray head and gaunt jaws works at his
          case,
He turns his quid of tobacco while his eyes blurr with the
          manuscript;
The malform'd limbs are tied to the surgeon's table,
What is removed drops horribly in a pail;
The quadroon girl is sold at the auction-stand, the drunkard
          nods by the bar-room stove,
The machinist rolls up his sleeves, the policeman travels his beat,
          the gate-keeper marks who pass,

The young fellow drives the express-wagon, (I love him, though
     I do not know him;)
The half-breed straps on his light boots to compete in the race,
The western turkey-shooting draws old and young, some lean
     on their rifles, some sit on logs,
Out from the crowd steps the marksman, takes his position,
     levels his piece,
The groups of newly-come immigrants cover the wharf or levee,
As the wooly-pates hoe in the sugar-field, the overseer views
     them from his saddle,
The bugle calls in the ball room, the gentlemen run for their
     partners, the dancers bow to each other,
The youth lies awake in the cedar-roof'd garret and harks to the
     musical rain,
The Wolverine sets traps on the creek that helps fill the Huron,
The squaw wrapt in her yellow-hemm'd cloth is offering
     moccasins and bead-bags for sale,
The connoisseur peers along the exhibition-gallery with
     half-shut eyes bent sideways,
As the deck-hands make fast the steamboat the plank is thrown
     for the shore-going passengers,
The young sister holds out the skein while the elder sister
     winds it off in a ball, and stops now and then for the
     knots,
The one-year wife is recovering and happy having a week ago
     borne her first child,
The clean-hair'd Yankee girl works with her sewing-machine or
     in the factory or mill,
The paving-man leans on his two-handed rammer, the
     reporter's lead flies swiftly over the note-book, the
     sign-painter is lettering with blue and gold.
The canal boy trots on the tow-path, the book-keeper counts at
     his desk, the shoemaker waxes his thread.
The conductor beats time for the band and all the performers
     follow him,
The child is baptized, the convert is making his first professions,
The regatta is spread on the bay, the race is begun, (how the
     white sails sparkle!)

The drover watching his drove sings out to them that would
        stray,
The pedler sweats with his pack on his back, (the purchaser
        higgling about the odd cent;)
The bride unrumples her white dress, the minute-hand of the
        clock moves slowly,
The opium-eater reclines with rigid head, just open'd lips,
The prostitute draggles her shawl, her bonnet bobs on her tipsy
        and pimpled neck,
The crowd laugh at her blackguard oaths, the men jeer and
        wink to each other,
(Miserable! I do not laugh at your oaths nor jeer you;)
The President holding a cabinet council is surrounded by the
        great Secretaries,
On the piazza walk three matrons stately and friendly with
        twined arms,
The crew of the fish-smack pack repeated layers of halibut in the
        hold,
The Missourian crosses the plains toting his wares and his cattle,
As the fare-collector goes through the train he gives notice by
        the jingling of loose change,
The floor-men are laying the floor, the tinners are tinning the
        roof, the masons are calling for mortar,
In single file each shouldering his hod pass onward the laborers;
Seasons pursuing each other the indescribable crowd is gather'd,
        it is the fourth of Seventh-month, (what salutes of cannon
        and small arms!)
Seasons pursuing each other the plougher ploughs, the mower
        mows, and the winter-grain falls in the ground;
Off on the lakes the pike-fisher watches and waits by the hole in
        the frozen surface,
The stumps stand thick round the clearing, the squatter strikes
        deep with his axe,
Flatboatmen make fast towards dusk near the cotton-wood or
        pecan-trees,
Coon-seekers go through the regions of the Red river or
        through those drain'd by the Tennessee, or through those
        of the Arkansas,

Torches shine in the dark that hangs on the Chattahooche or
        Altamahaw,
Patriarchs sit at supper with sons and grandsons and great
        grandsons around them,
In walls of adobie, in canvas tents, rest hunters and trappers
        after their day's sport,
The city sleeps and the country sleeps,
The living sleep for their time, the dead sleep for their time,
The old husband sleeps by his wife and the young husband
        sleeps by his wife;
And these tend inward to me, and I tend outward to them,
And such as it is to be of these more or less I am,
And of these one and all I weave the song of myself.

16

I am of old and young, of the foolish as much as the wise,
Regardless of others, ever regardful of others,
Maternal as well as paternal, a child as well as a man,
Stuff'd with the stuff that is coarse and stuff'd with the stuff that
        is fine,
One of the Nation of many nations, the smallest the same and
        the largest the same,
A Southerner soon as a Northerner, a planter nonchalant and
        hospitable down by the Oconee I live,
A Yankee bound my own way ready for trade, my joints the
        limberest joints on earth and the sternest joints on earth,
A Kentuckian walking the vale of the Elkhorn in my deerskin
        leggings, a Louisianian or Georgian,
A boatman over lakes or bays or along coasts, a Hoosier, Badger,
        Buckeye;
At home on Kanadian snow-shoes or up in the bush, or with
        fishermen off Newfoundland,
At home in the fleet of ice-boats, sailing with the rest and
        tacking,
At home on the hills of Vermont or in the woods of Maine, or
        the Texan ranch,
Comrade of Californians, comrade of free North-Westerners,
        (loving their big proportions,)

Comrade of raftsmen and coalmen, comrade of all who shake
     hands and welcome to drink and meat,
A learner with the simplest, a teacher of the thoughtfullest,
A novice beginning yet experient of myriads of seasons,
Of every hue and cast am I, of every rank and religion,
A farmer, mechanic, artist, gentleman, sailor, quaker,
Prisoner, fancy-man, rowdy, lawyer, physician, priest.

I resist any thing better than my own diversity,
Breathe the air but leave plenty after me,
And am not stuck up, and am in my place.

(The moth and the fish-eggs are in their place,
The bright suns I see and the dark suns I cannot see are in their
     place,
The palpable is in its place and the impalpable in its place.)

17

These are really the thoughts of all men in all ages and lands,
     they are not original with me,
If they are not yours as much as mine they are nothing, or next
     to nothing.
If they are not the riddle and the untying of the riddle they are
     nothing,
If they are not just as close as they are distant they are nothing.

This is the grass that grows wherever the land is and the water
     is,
This the common air that bathes the globe.

18

With music strong I come, with my cornets and my drums,
I play not marches for accepted victors only, I play marches for
     conquer'd and slain persons.

Have you heard that it was good to gain the day?
I also say it is good to fall, battles are lost in the same spirit in

which they are won.

I beat and pound for the dead,
I blow through my embouchures my loudest and gayest for
them.

Vivas to those who have fail'd
And to those whose war-vessels sank in the sea!
And to those themselves who sank in the sea!

And to all generals that lost engagements, and all overcome
heroes!

And the numberless unknown heroes equal to the greatest
heroes known!

19

This is the meal equally set, this the meat for natural hunger,
It is for the wicked just the same as the righteous, I make
appointments with all,
I will not have a single person slighted or left away,
The kept-woman, sponger, thief, are hereby invited,
The heavy-lipp'd slave is invited, the venerealee is invited;
There shall be no difference between them and the rest.

This is the press of a bashful hand, this the float and odor of
hair,
This the touch of my lips to yours, this the murmur of yearning,
This the far-off depth and height reflecting my own face,
This the thoughtful merge of myself, and the outlet again.

Do you guess I have some intricate purpose?
Well I have, for the Fourth-month showers have, and the mica
on the side of a rock has.
Do you take it I would astonish?
Does the daylight astonish? does the early redstart twittering
through the woods?
Do I astonish more than they?

This hour I tell things in confidence,
I might not tell everybody, but I will tell you.

20

Who goes there? hankering, ross, mystical, nude;
How is it I extract strength from the beef I eat?

What is a man anyhow? what am I? what are you?

All I mark as my own you shall offset it with your own,
Else it were time lost listening to me.

I do not snivel that snivel the world over,
The months are vacuums and the ground but wallow and filth.

Whimpering and truckling fold with powders for invalids, con-
        formity goes to the fourth-remov'd,
I wear my hat as I please indoors or out.

Why should I pray? why should I venerate and be ceremonious?

Having pried through the strata, analyzed to a hair, counsel'd
        with doctors and calculated close,
I find no sweeter fat than sticks to my own bones.

In all people I see myself; none more and not one a barley-corn
        less,
And the good or bad I say of myself I say of them.

I know I am solid and sound,
To me the converging objects of the universe perpetually flow,
All are written to me, and I mut get what the writing means.

I know I am deathless,
I know this orbit of mine cannot be swept by a carpenter's com-
        pass,
I know I shall not pass like a child's carlacue cut with a burnt
        stick at night.

I know I am august,
I do not trouble my spirit to vindicate itself or be understood,
I see that the elementary laws never apologize,
(I reckon I behave no prouder than the level I plant my house
        by, after all.)

I exist as I am, that is enough,
If no other in the world be aware I am content,
And if each and all be aware I sit content. .
One world is aware and by far the largest to me, and that is
        myself,
And whether I come to my own to-day or in ten thousand or ten
        million years,
I can cheerfully take it now, or with equal cheerfulness I can
        wait.

My foothold is tenon'd and mortis'd in granite,
I laugh at what you call dissolution,
And I know the amplitude of time.

21

I am the poet of the Body and I am the poet of the Soul,
The pleasures of heaven are with me and the pains of hell are
        with me,
The first I graft and increase upon myself, the latter I translate
        into a new tongue.

I am the poet of the woman the same as the man,
And I say it is as great to be a woman as to be a man,
And I say there is nothing greater than the mother of men.

I chant the chant of dilation or pride,
We have had ducking and deprecating about enough,
I show that size is only development.
Have you outstript the rest? are you the President?
It is a trifle, they will more than arrive there every one, and still
        pass on.
I am he that walks with the tender and growing night,

I call to the earth and sea half-held by the night.

Press close bare-bosom'd night—press close magnetic nourishing
        night!
Night of south winds—night of the large few stars!
Still nodding night—made naked summer night.

Smile O voluptuous cool-breath'd earth!
Earth of the slumbering and liquid trees!
Earth of departed sunset—earth of the mountains misty-topt!
Earth of the vitreous pour of the full moon just tinged with
        blue!
Earth of shine and dark mottling the tide of the river!
Earth of the limpid gray of clouds brighter and clearer for my
        sake!
Far-swooping elbow'd earth—rich apple-blossom'd earth!
Smile, for your lover comes.

Prodigal, you have given me love—therefore I to you give love!
O unspeakable passionate love.

You sea! I resign myself to you also—I guess what you mean,
I behold from the beach your crooked inviting fingers.

22

I believe you refuse to go back without feeling of me,
We must have a turn together, I undress, hurry me out of sight
        of the land,
Cushion me soft, rock me in billowy drowse,
Dash me with amorous wet, I can repay you.

Sea of stretch'd ground-swells,
Sea breathing broad and convulsive breaths,
Sea of the brine of life and of unshovel'd yet always-ready
        graves,
Howler and scooper of storms, capricious and dainty sea,
I am integral with you, I too am of one phase and of all phases.

Partaker of influx and efflux, I, extoller of hate and
    conciliation,
Extoller of amies and those that sleep in each other's arms,
I am he attesting sympathy,
(Shall I make my list of things in the house and skip the house
    that supports them?)

I am not the poet of goodness only, I do not decline to be the
    poet of wickedness also.

What blurt is this about virtue and about vice?
Evil propels me and reform of evil propels me, I stand
    indifferent,
My gait is no fault-finder's or rejecter's gait,
I moisten the roofs of all that has grown.

Did you fear some scrofula out of the unflagging pregnancy?
Did you guess the celestial laws are yet to be work'd over and
    rectified?

I find one side a balance and the antipodal side a balance,
Soft doctrine as steady help as stable doctrine,
Thoughts and deeds of the present our rouse and early start.

This minute that comes to me over the past decillions,
There is no better than it and now.

What behaved well in the past or behaves well to-day is not such
    a wonder,
The wonder is always and always how there can be a mean man
    or an infidel.

23

Endless unfolding of words of ages!
And mine a word of the modern, the word En-Mass.

A word of the faith that never balks,
Here or henceforward it is all the same to me, I accept Time
      absolutely.
It alone is without flaw, it alone rounds and completes all,
That mystic baffling wonder alone completes all.

I accept Reality and dare not question it,
Materialism first and last imbuing.

Hurrah for positive science! long live exact demonstration!
Fetch stonecrop mixt with cedar and branches of lilac,
This is the lexicographer, this the chemist, this made a grammar
      of the old cartouches,
These mariners put the ship through dangerous unknown seas,
This is the geologist, this works with the scalpel, and this is a
      mathematician.

Gentlemen, to you the first honors always!
Your facts are useful, and yet they are not my dwelling,
I but enter by them to an area of my dwelling.

Less the reminders of properties told my words,
And more the reminders they of life untold, and of freedom
      and extrication,
And make short account of neuters and geldings, and favor men
      and women fully equipt,
And beat the gong of revolt, and stop with fugitives and them
      that plot and conspire.

24

Walt Whitman, a kosmos, of Manhattan the son,
Turbulent, fleshy, sensual, eating, drinking and breeding,

No sentimentalist, no stander above men and women or apart
        from them,
No more modest than immodest.

Unscrew the locks from the doors!
Unscrew the doors themselves from their jambs!

Whoever degrades another degrades me,
And whatever is done or said returns at last to me.

Through me the afflatus surging and surging, through me the
        current and index.

I speak the pass-word primeval, I give the sign of democracy,
By God! I will accept nothing which all cannot have their
        counterpart of on the same terms.

Through me many long dumb voices,
Voices of the interminable generations of prisoners and slaves,
Voices of the diseas'd and despairing and of thieves and dwarfs,
Voices of cycles of preparation and accretion,
And of the threads that connect the stars, and of wombs and of
        the father-stuff,
And of the rights of them the others are down upon,
Of the deform'd, trivial, flat, foolish, despised,
Fog in the air, beetles rolling balls of dung.

Through me forbidden voices,
Voices of sexes and lusts, voices veil'd and I remove the veil,
Voices indecent by me clarified and transfigur'd.
I do not press my fingers across my mouth,
I keep as delicate around the bowels as around the head and
        heart,
Copulation is no more rank to me than death is.

I believe in the flesh and the appetites,
Seeing, hearing, feeling, are miracles, and each part and tag of
        me is a miracle.

Divine am I inside and out, and I make holy whatever I touch or
    am touch'd from,
The scent of these arm-pits aroma finer than prayer,
This head more than churches, bibles, and all the creeds.

If I worship one thing more than another it shall be the spread
    of my own body, or any part of it,
Translucent mould of me it shall be you!
Shaded ledges and rests it shall be you!
Firm masculine colter it shall be you!
Whatever goes to the tilth of me it shall be you!
You my rich blood! your milky stream pale strippings of my life!
Breast that presses against other breasts it shall be you!
My brain it shall be your occult convolutions!
Root of wash'd sweet-flag! timorous pond-snipe! nest of guarded
    duplicate eggs! it shall be you!
Mix'd tussled hay of head, beard, brawn, it shall be you!
Trickling sap of maple, fibre of manly wheat, it shall be you!
Sun so generous it shall be you!
Vapors lighting and shading my face it shall be you!
You sweaty brooks and dews it shall be you!
Winds whose soft-tickling genitals rub against me it shall be you!
Broad muscular fields, branches of live oak, loving lounger in
    my winding paths, it shall be you!
Hands I have taken, face I have kiss'd, mortal I have ever
    touch'd, it shall be you.

I dote on myself, there is that lot of me and all so luscious,
Each moment and whatever happens thrills me with joy,
I cannot tell how my ankles bend, nor whence the cause of my
    faintest wish,
Nor the cause of the friendship I emit, nor the cause of the
    friendship I take again.

That I walk up my stoop, I pause to consider if it really be,
A morning-glory at my window satisfies me more than the
    metaphysics of books.

To behold the day break!

The little light fades the immense and diaphanous shadows,
The air tastes good to my palate.

Hefts of the moving world at innocent gambols silently rising,
      freshly exuding,
Scooting obliquely high and low.

Something I cannot see puts upward libidinous prongs,
Seas of bright juice suffuse heaven.

The earth by the sky staid with, the daily close of their junction,
The heav'd challenge from the east that moment over my head,
The mocking taunt, See then whether you shall be master!

25

Dazzling and tremendous how quick he sun-rise would kill me,
If I could not now and always send sun-rise out of me.

We also ascend dazzling and tremendous as the sun,
We found our own O my soul in the calm and cool of the
      daybreak.

My voice goes after what my eyes cannot reach,
With the twirl of my tongue I encompass worlds and volumes of
      worlds.

Speech is the twin of my vision, it is unequal to measure itself,
It provokes me forever, it says sarcastically,
Walt you contain enough, why don't you let it out then?

Come now I will not be tantalized, you conceive too much of
      articulation,
Do you not know O speech how the buds beneath you are
      folded?
Waiting in gloom, protected by frost,
The dirt receding before my prophetical screams,
I underlying causes to balance them at last,

My knowledge my live parts, it keeping tally with the meaning of
    all things,
Happiness, (which whoever hears me let him or her set out in
    search of this day.)
My final merit I refuse you, I refuse putting from me what I
    really am,
Encompass worlds, but never try to encompass me,
I crowd your sleekest and best by simply looking toward you.

Writing and talk do not prove me,
I carry the plenum of proof and every thing else in my face,
With the hush of my lips I wholly confound the skeptic.

26

Now I will do nothing but listen,
To accrue what I hear into this song, to let sounds contribute
    toward it.
I hear bravuras of birds, bustle of growing wheat, gossip of
    flames, clack of sticks cooking my meals,
I hear the sound of love, the sound of the human voice,
I hear all sounds running together, combined, fused or
    following,
Sounds of the city and sounds out of the city, sounds of the
    day and night,
Talkative young ones to those that like them, the loud laugh of
    workingpeople at their meals,
The angry base of disjointed friendship, the faint tones of the
    sick,
The judge with hands tight to the desk, his pallid lips
    pronouncing a death-sentence,
The heave'yo of stevedores unlading ships by the wharves, the
    refrain of the anchor-lifters,
The ring of alarm-bells, the cry of fire, the whirr of
    swift streaking engines and hose-carts with premonitory
    tinkles and color'd lights,
The steam-whistle, the solid roll of the train of approaching
    cars,

The slow march play'd at the head of the association marching
  two and two,
(They go to guard some corpse, the flag-tops are draped with
  black muslin.)

I hear the violoncello, ('tis the young man's heart's complaint,)
I hear the key'd cornet, it glides quickly in through my ears.
It shakes mad-sweet pangs through my belly and breast.

I hear the chorus, it is a grand opera,
Ah this indeed is music—this suits me.

A tenor large and fresh as the creation fills me,
The orbic flex of his mouth is pouring and filling me full.

I hear the train'd soprano (what work with hers is this?)
The orchestra whirls me wider than Uranus flies,
It wrenches such ardors from me I did not know I possess'd
  them,
It sails me, I dab with bare feet, they are lick'd by the indolent
  waves,
I am cut by bitter and angry hail, I lose my breath,
Steep'd amid honey'd morphine, my windpipe throttled in fakes
  of death,
At length let up again to feel the puzzle of puzzles,
And that we call Being.

27

To be in any form, what is that?
(Round and round we go, all of us, and ever come back thither,)
If nothing lay more develop'd the quahaug in its callous shell
  were enough.

Mine is no callous shell,
I have instant conductors all over me whether I pass or stop,
They seize every object and lead it harmlessly through me.

I merely stir, press, feel with my fingers, and am happy,

To touch my person to some one else's is about as much as I
    can stand.

28

Is this then a touch? quivering me to a new identity,
Flames and ether making a rush for my veins,
Treacherous tip of me reaching and crowding to help them,
My flesh and blood playing out lightning to strike what is hardly
    different from myself,
On all sides prurient provokers stiffening my limbs,
Straining the udder of my heart for its withheld drip,
Behaving licentious toward me, taking no denial,
Depriving me of my bet as for a purpose,
Unbuttoning my clothes, holding me by the bare waist,
Deluding my confusion with the calm of the sunlight and
    pasture-fields,
Immodestly sliding the fellow-senses away,
They bribed to swap off with touch and go and graze at the
    edges of me,
No consideration, no regard for my draining strength or my
    anger,
Fetching the rest of the herd around to enjoy them a while,
Then all uniting to stand on a headland and worry me.

The sentries desert every other part of me,
They have left me helpless to a red marauder,
They all come to the headland to witness and assist against me.

I am given up by traitors,
I talk wildly, I have lost my wits, I and nobody else am the
    greatest traitor,
I went myself first to the headland, my own hands carried me
    there.
Your villian touch! what are you doing? my breath is tight in its
    throat,
Unclench your floodgates, you are too much for me.

29

Blind loving wrestling touch, sheath'd hooded sharp-tooth'd
    touch!
Did it make you ache so, leaving me?
Parting track'd by arriving, perpetual payment of perpetual
    loan,
Rich showering rain, and recompense richer afterward.

Sprouts take and accumulate, stand by the curb prolific and
    vital,
Landscapes projected masculine, full-sized and golden.

30

All truths wait in all things,
They neither hasten their own delivery nor resist it,
They do not need the obstetric forceps of the surgeon,
The insignificant is as big to me as any,
(What is less or more than a touch?)

Logic and sermons never convince,
The damp of the night drives deeper into my soul.

(Only what proves itself to every man and woman is so,
Only what nobody denies is so.)

A minute and a drop of me settle my brain,
I believe the soggy clods shall become lovers and lamps,
And a compend of compends is the meat of a man or woman,
And a summit and flower there is the feeling they have for each
    other,
And they are to branch boundlessly out of that lesson until it
    became omnific,
And until one and all shall delight us, and we them.

31

I believe a leaf of grass is no less than the journey-work of the
    stars,

And the pismire is equally perfect, and a grain of sand, and the
        egg of the wren,
And the tree-toad is a chef-d'oeuvre for the highest,
And the running blackberry would adorn the parlors of heaven,
And the narrowest hinge in my hand puts to scorn all
        machinery,
And the cow crunching with depress'd head surpasses any
        statue,
And a mouse is miracle enough to stagger sextillions of infidels.

I find I incorporate gneiss, coal, long-threaded moss, fruits,
        grains, esculent roots,
And am stucco'd with quadrupeds and birds all over,
And have distanced what is behind me for good reasons,
But call any thing back again when I desire it.

In vain the speeding or shyness,
In vain the plutonic rocks send their old heat against my
        approach,
In vain the mastodon retreats beneath its own powder'd bones,
In vain objects stand leagues off and assume manifold shapes,
In vain the ocean settling in hollows and the great monsters
        lying low,
In vain the buzzard houses herself with the sky,
In vain the snake slides through the creepers and logs,
In vain the elk takes to the inner passes of the woods,
In vain the razor-bill'd auk sails far north to Labrador,
I follow quickly, I ascend to the nest in the fissure of the cliff.

32

I think I could turn and live with animals, they're so placid and
        self-contain'd,
I stand and look at them long and long.

They do not sweat and whine about their condition,
They do not lie awake in the dark and weep for their sins,
They do not make me sick discussing their duty to God,

Not one is dissatisfied, not one is demented with the mania of
    owning things,
Not one kneels to another, nor to his kind that lived thousands
    of years ago,
Not one is respectable or unhappy over the whole earth.
So they show their relations to me and I accept them,
They bring me tokens of myself, they evince them plainly in
    their possession.

I wonder where they get those tokens,
Did I pass that way huge times ago and negligently drop them?

Myself moving forward then and now and forever,
Gathering and showing more always and with velocity,
Infinite and omnigenous, and the like of these among them,
Not too exclusive toward the reachers of my remembrancers,
Picking out here one that I love, and now go with him on
    brotherly terms.

A gigantic beauty of a stallion, fresh and responsive to my
    caresses,
Head high in the forehead, wide between the ears,
Limbs glossy and supple, tail dusting the ground,
Eyes full of sparkling wickedness, ears finely cut, flexibly
    moving.

His nostrils dilate as my heels embrace him,
His well-built limbs tremble with pleasure as we race around and
    return,
I but use you a minute, then I resign you, stallion,
Why do I need your paces when I myself out-gallop them?
Even as I stand or sit passing faster than you.

33

Space and Time! now I see it is true, what I guess'd at,
What I guess'd when I loaf'd on the grass,
What I guess'd while I lay alone in my bed,

And again as I walk'd the beach under the paling stars of the
        morning.

My ties and ballasts leave me, my elbows rest in sea-gaps,
I skirt sierras, my palms cover continents,
I am afoot with my vision.

By the city's quadrangular houses—in log huts, camping with
        lumbermen,
Along the ruts of the turnpike, along the dry gulch and rivulet
        bed,
Weeding my onion-patch or hoeing rows of carrots and
        parsnips, crossing savannas, trailing in forests,
Prospecting, gold-digging, girdling the trees of a new purchase,
Scorch'd ankle-deep by the hot sand, hauling my boat down the
        shallow river,
Where the panther walks to and fro on a limb overhead, where
        the buck turns furiously at the hunter,
Where the rattlesnake suns his flabby length on a rock, where
        the otter is feeding on fish,
Where the alligator in his tough pimples sleeps by the bayou;
Where the black bear is searching for roots or honey, where
        the beaver pats the mud with his paddle-shaped tail;
Over the growing sugar, over the yellow-flower'd cotton plant,
        over the rice in its low moist field,
Over the sharp-peak'd farm house, with its scallop'd scum and
        slender shoots from the gutters,
Over the western persimmon, over the long-leav'd corn, over
        the delicate blue-flower flax,
Over the white and brown buckwheat, a hummer and buzzer
        there with the rest,
Over the dusky green of the rye as it ripples and shades in the
        breeze;
Scaling mountains, pulling myself cautiously up, holding on by
        low scragged limbs,
Walking the path worn in the grass and beat through the leaves
        of the brush,
Where the quail is whistling betwixt the woods and the
        wheat-lot,

Where the bat flies in the Seventh-month eve, where the great
    goldbug drops through the dark,
Where the brook puts out of the roots of the old tree and flows
    to the meadow,
Where cattle stand and shake away flies with the tremulous
    shuddering of their hides,
Where the cheese-cloth hangs in the kitchen, where andirons
    straddle the hearth-slab, where cobwebs fall in festoons
    from the rafters;
Where trip-hammers crash, where the press is whirling its
    cylinders,
Where the human heart beats with terrible throes under its
    ribs,
Where the pear-shaped balloon is floating aloft, (floating in it
    myself and looking composedly down,)
Where the life-car is drawn on the slip-noose, where the heat
    hatches pale-green eggs in the dented sand,
Where the she-whale swims with her calf and never forsakes it,
Where the steam-ship trails hind-ways its long pennant of
    smoke,
Where the fin of the shark cuts like a black chip out of the
    water,
Where the half-burn'd brig is riding on unknown currents,
Where shells grow to her slimy deck, where the dead are
    corrupting below;
Where the dense-starr'd flag is borne at the head of the
    regiments,
Approaching Manhattan up by the long-stretching island,
Under Niagara, the cataract falling like a veil over my
    countenance,
Upon a door-step, upon the horse-block of hard wood outside,
Upon the race-course, or enjoying picnics or jigs or a good
    game of base-ball,
At he-festivals, with blackguard jibes, ironical license,
    bull-dances, drinking, laughter,
At the cider-mill tasting the sweets of the brown mash, sucking
    the juice through a straw.
At apple-peelings wanting kisses for all the red fruit I find,
At musters, beach-parties, friendly bees, huskings,

house-raisings,
Where the mocking-bird sounds his delicious gurgles, cackles,
          screams, weeps,
Where the hay-rick stands in the barn-yard, where the
          dry-stalks are scatter'd, where the broad-cow waits in
          the hovel,
Where the bull advances to do his masculine work, where the
          stud to the mare, where the cock is treading the hen,
Where the heifers browse, where geese nip their food with
          short jerks,
Where sun-down shadows lengthen over the limitless and
          lonesome prairie,
Where herds of buffalo make a crawling spread of the square
          miles far and near,
Where the humming-bird shimmers, where the neck of the
          long-lived swam is curving and winding,
Where the laughing-gull scoots by the shore, where she laughs
          her near-human laugh,
Where bee-hives range on a gray bench in the garden half hid
          by the high weeds,
Where band-neck'd partridges roost in a ring on the ground
          with their heads out,
Where burial coaches enter the arch'd gates of a cemetery,
Where winter wolves bark amid wastes of snow and icicled
          trees,
Where the yellow-crown'd heron comes to the edge of the
          marsh at night and feeds upon small crabs,
Where the splash of swimmers and divers cools the warm noon,
Where the katy-did works her chromatic reed on the
          walnut-tree over the well,
Through patches of citrons and cucumbers with silver-wired
          leaves,
Through the salt-lick or orange glade, or under conical firs,
Through the gymnasium, through the curtain'd saloon,
          through the office or public hall;
Pleas'd with the native and pleas'd with the foreign, pleas'd
          with the new and old,
Pleas'd with the homely woman as well as the handsome,

Pleas'd with the quakeress as she puts off her bonnet and talks
        melodiously,
Pleas'd with the tune of the choir of the whitewash'd church,
Pleas'd with the earnest words of the sweating Methodist
        preacher, impress'd seriously at the camp-meeting;
Looking in at the shop-windows of Broadway the whole
        forenoon, flatting the flesh of my nose on the thick plate
        glass,
Wandering the same afternoon with my face turn'd up to the
        clouds, or down a lane or along the beach,
My right and left arms round the sides of two friends, and I in
        the middle;
Coming home with the silent and dark-cheek'd bush-boy,
        (behind me he rides at the drape of the day,)
Far from the settlements studying the print of animals' feet, or
        the moccasin print,
By the cot in the hospital reaching lemonade to a feverish
        patient,
Nigh the coffin'd corpse when all is still, examining with a
        candle;
Voyaging to every port to dicker and adventure,
Hurrying with the modern crowd as eager and fickle as any,
Hot toward one I hate, ready in my madness to knife him,
Solitary at midnight in my back yard, my thoughts gone from
        me a long while,
Walking the old hills of Judæa with the beautiful gentle God by
        my side,
Speeding through space, speeding through heaven and the
        stars,
Speeding amid the seven satellites and the broad ring, and the
        diameter of eighty thousand miles,
Speeding with tail'd meteors, throwing fire-balls like the rest,
Carrying the cresent child that carries its own full mother in
        its belly,
Storming, enjoying, planning, loving, cautioning,
Backing and filling, appearing and disappearing,
I tread day and night such roads.

I visit the orchards of spheres and look at the product,

and look at quintillions ripen'd and look at quintillions green.

I fly those flights of a fluid and swallowing soul,
My course runs below the soundings of plummets.

I help myself to material and immaterial,
No guard can shut me off, no law prevent me.

I anchor my ship for a little while only,
My messengers continually cruise away or bring their returns to
        me.

I go hunting polar furs and the seal, leaping chasms with a
        pike-pointed staff, clinging to topples of brittle and blue.

I ascend to the foretruck,
I take my place late at night in the crow's-nest,
We sail the arctic sea, it is plenty light enough,
Through the clear atmosphere I stretch around on the
        wonderful beauty,
The enormous masses of ice pass me and I pass them, the
        scenery is plain in all directions,
The white-topt mountains show in the distance, I fling out my
        fancies toward them,
We are approaching some great battle-field in which we are
        soon to be engaged,
We pass the colossal outposts of the encampment, we pass with
        still feet and caution,
Or we are entering by the suburbs some vast and ruin'd city,
The blocks and fallen architecture more than all the living
        cities of the globe.

I am a free companion, I bivouac by invading watchfires,
I turn the bridegroom out of bed and stay with the bride
        myself,
I tighten her all night to my thighs and lips.

My voice is the wife's voice, the screech by the rail of the stairs,
They fetch my man's body up dripping and drown'd.

I understand the large hearts of heroes,
The courage of present times and all times,
How the skipper saw the crowded and rudderless wreck of the
      steamship, and Death chasing it up and down the storm,
How he knuckled tight and gave not back an inch, and was
      faithful of days and faithful of nights,
And chalk'd in large letters on a board, *Be of good cheer, we will*
      not desert you;
How he follow'd with them and tack'd with them three days
      and would not give it up,
How he saved the drifting company at last,
How the lank loose-gown'd women look'd when boated from
      the side of their prepared graves,
How the silent old-faced infants and the lifted sick, and the
      sharp-lipp'd unshaved men;
All this I swallow, it tastes good, I like it well, it becomes mine,
I am the man, I suffer'd, I was there.
The disdain and calmness of martyrs,
The mother of old, condemn'd for a witch, burnt with dry
      wood, her children gazing on,
The hounded slave that flags in the race, leans by the fence,
      blowing cover'd with sweat,
The twinges that sting like needles his legs and neck, the
      murderous buckshot and the bullets,
All these I feel I am.

I am the hounded slave, I wince at the bite of the dogs,
Hell and despair are upon me, crack and again crack the
      marksmen,
I clutch the rails of the fence, my gore dribs, thinn'd with the
      ooze of my skin,
I fall on the weeds and stones,
The riders spur their unwilling horses, haul close,
Taunt my dizzy ears and beat me violently over the head with
      whipstocks.

Agonies are one of my changes of garments.
I do not ask the wounded person how he feels, I myself
      become the wounded person,

My hurts turn livid upon me as I lean on a cane and observe.

I am the mash'd fireman with breast-bone broken,
Tumbling walls buried me in their depris,
Heat and smoke I inspired, I heard the yelling shouts of my
          comrades,
I heard the distant click of their picks and shovels,
They have clear'd the beams away, they tenderly lift me forth.

I lie in the night air in my red shirt, the pervading hush is for
          my sake,
Painless after all I lie exhausted but not so unhappy,
White and beautiful are the faces around me, the heads are
          bared of their fire-caps,
The kneeling crowd fades with the light of the torches.

Distant and dead resuscitate,
They show me as the dial or move as the hands of me, I am
          the clock myself.

I am the old artillerist, I tell of my fort's bombardment,
I am there again.

Again the long roll of the drummers,
Again the attacking cannon, mortars,
Again to my listening ears the cannon responsive.

I take part, I see and hear the whole,
The cries, curses, roar, the plaudits for well-aim'd shots,
The ambulanza slowly passing trailing its red drip,
Workmen searching after damages, making indispensable
          repairs,
The fall of grenades through the rent roof, the fan-shaped
          explosion,
The whizz of limbs, heads, stone, wood, iron, high in the air.

Again gurgles the mouth of my dying general, he furiously
          waves with his hand,
He gasps through the clot *Mind me not—mind—the entrenchments.*

34

Now I tell what I knew in Texas in my early youth,
(I tell not the fall of Alamo,
No one escaped to tell the fall of Alamo,
The hundred and fifty are dumb yet at Alamo,)
'Tis the tale of the murder in cold blood of four hundred and
        twelve young men.

Retreating they had form'd in a hollow square with their
            baggage for breastworks,
Nine hundred lives out of the surrounding enemy's nine times
            their number, was the price they took in advance,
Their colonel was wounded and their ammunition gone,
They treated for an honorable capitulation, receiv'd writing
            and seal, gave up their arms and march'd back prisoners
            of war.

They were the glory of the race of rangers,
Matchless with horse, rifle, song, supper, courtship,
Large, turbulent, generous, handsome, proud, and affectionate,
Bearded, sunburnt, drest in the free costume of hunters,
Not a single one over thirty years of age.

The second First-day morning they were brought out in squads
            and massacred, it was beautiful early summer,
The work commenced about five o'clock and was over by eight.

None obey'd the command to kneel,
Some made a mad and helpless rush, some stood stark and
            straight,
A few fell at once, shot in the temple or heart, the living and
            dead lay together,
The maim'd and mangled dug in the dirt, the new-comers saw
            them there,
Some half-kill'd attempted to crawl away,
These were despatch'd with bayonets or batter'd with the blunts
            of muskets.
A youth not seventeen years old seiz'd his assassin till two more

came to release him,
The three were all torn and cover'd with the boy's blood.

At eleven o'clock began the burning of the bodies;
This is the tale of the murder of the four hundred and twelve
        young men.

35

Would you hear of an old-time sea-fight?
Would you learn who won by the light of the moon and stars?
List the yarn, as my grandmother's father the sailor told it
        to me.

Our foe was no skulk in his ship I tell you, (said he,)
His was the surly English pluck, and there is no tougher or
        truer, and never was, and never will be;
Along the lower'd eve he came horribly raking us.

We closed with him, the yards entangled, the cannon touch'd,
My captain lash'd fast with his own hands.

We had receiv'd some eighteen pound shots under the water,
On our lower-gun deck two large pieces had burst at the first
        fire, killing all around and blowing up overhead.

Fighting at sun-down, fighting at dark
Ten o'clock at night, the full moon well up, our leaks on the
        gain, and five feet of water reported,
The master-at-arms loosing the prisoners confined in the
        after-hold to give them a chance for themselves.

The transmit to and from the magazine is now stopt by the
        sentinels,
They see so many strange faces they do not know whom to
        trust.

Our frigate takes fire,
The other asks if we demand quarter?

If our colors are struck and the fighting done?

Now I laugh content, for I hear the voice of my little captain,
We have not struck, he composedly cries, *we have just begun our
         part of the fighting.*

Only three guns are in use,
One is directed by the captain himself against the enemy's
         main-mast,
Two well serv'd with grape and canister silence his musketry
         and clear his decks.

The tops alone second the fire of this little battery, especially
         the main-top,
They hold out bravely during the whole of the action.

Not a moment's cease,
The leaks gain fast on the pumps, the fire eats toward the
         powder-magazine.

One of the pumps has been shot away, it is generally thought
         we are sinking.
Serene stands the little captain,
He is not hurried, his voice is neither high nor low,
His eyes give more light to us than our battle lanterns.

Toward twelve there in the beams of the moon they surrender
         to us.

36

Stretch'd and still lies the midnight,
Two great hulls motionless on the breast of the darkness,
Our vessel riddled and slowly sinking, preparations to pass to
         the one we have conquer'd,
The captain on the quarter-deck coldly giving his orders
         through a countenance white as a sheet,
Near by the corpse of the child that serv'd in the cabin,

The dead face of an old salt with long white hair and carefully
        curl'd whiskers,
The flames spite of all that can be done flickering aloft and
        below,
The husky voices of the two or three officers yet fit for duty,
Formless stacks of bodies and bodies by themselves, dabs of
        flesh upon the masts and spars,
Cut of cordage, dangle of rigging, slight shock of the soothe of
        waves,
Black and impassive guns, litter of powder-parcels, strong
        scent,
A few large stars overhead, silent and mournful shining,
Delicate sniffs of sea-breeze, smells of sedgy grass and fields by
        the shore, death-messages given in charge to survivors,
The hiss of the surgeon's knife, the gnawing teeth of his saw,
Wheeze, cluck, swash of falling blood, short wild scream, and
        long, dull, tapering groan,
These so, these irretrievable.

                                    37

You laggards there on guard! look to your arms!
In at the conquer'd doors they crowd! I am possess'd!
Embody all presences outlaw'd or suffering,
See myself in prison shaped like another man,
And feel the dull unintermitted pain.

For me the keepers of convicts shoulder their carbines and
        keep watch,
It is I let out in the morning and barr'd at night.

Not a mutineer walks handcuff'd to jail but I am handcuff'd to
        him and walk by his side,
(I am less the jolly one there, and more the silent one with
        sweat on my twitching lips.)

Not a youngster is taken for larceny but I go up too, and am
        tried and sentenced.

Not a cholera patient lies at the last gasp but I also lie at the
      last gasp,
My face is ash-color'd, my sinews gnarl, away from me people
      retreat.

Askers embody themselves in me and I am embodied in them,
I project my hat, sit shame-faced, and beg.

38

Enough! enough! enough!
Somehow I have been stunn'd. Stand back!
Give me a little time beyond my duff'd head, slumbers, dreams,
      gaping,
I discover myself on the verge of a usual mistake.

That I could forget the mockers and insults!
That I could forget the trickling tears and the blows of the
      bludgeons and hammers!
That I could look with a separate look on my own crucifixion
      and bloody crowning!

I remember now,
I resume the overstaid fraction,
The grave of rock multiplies what has been confined to it, or to
      any graves,
Corpses rise, gashes heal, fastenings roll from me.

I troop forth replenish'd with supreme power, one of an
      average unending procession,
Inland and sea-coast we go, and pass all boundary lines,
Our swift ordinances on their way over the whole earth,
The blossoms we wear in our hats the growth of thousands of
      years.

Eleves, I salute you! come forward!
Continue your annotations, continue your questionings.

39

The friendly and flowing savage, who is he?
Is he waiting for civilization, or past it and mastering it?

Is he some Southwesterner rais'd out-doors? is he Kanadian?
Is he from the Mississippi country? Iowa, Oregon, California?
The mountains? prairie-life, bush-life? or sailor from the sea?

Wherever he goes men and women accept and desire him,
They desire he should like them, touch them, speak to them,
          stay with them.

Behavior lawless as snow-flakes, words simple as grass,
          uncomb'd head, laughter, and naiveté,
Slow-stepping feet, common features, common modes and
          emanations,
They descend in new forms from the tips of his fingers,
The are wafted with the odor of his body or breath, they fly out
          of the glance of his eyes.

40

Flaunt of the sunshine I need not your bask—lie over!
You light surface only, I force surfaces and depths also.

Earth! you seem to look for something at my hands,
Say, old top-knot, what do you want?

Man or woman, I might tell how I like you, but cannot,
And might tell what it is in me and what it is in you, but
          cannot,
And might tell that pining I have, that pulse of my nights and
          days.

Behold, I do not give lectures or a little charity,
When I give I give myself.

You there, impotent, loose in the knees,
Open your scarf'd chops till I blow grit within you,
Spread your palms and lift the flaps of your pockets,
I am not to be denied, I compel, I have stores plenty and to
        spare,
And any thing I have I bestow.

I do not ask who you are, that is not important to me,
You can do nothing and be nothing but what I will infold you.

To cotton-field drudge or cleaner of privies I lean,
On his right cheek I put the family kiss,
And in my soul I swear I never will deny him.

On women fit for conception I start bigger and nimbler babes,
(This day I am jetting the stuff of far more arrogant republics.)

To any one dying, thither I speed and twist the knob of the
        door,
Turn the bed-clothes toward the foot of the bed,
Let the physician and the priest go home.

I seize the descending man and raise him with resistless will,
O despairer, here is my neck,
By God, you shall not go down! hang your whole weight upon
        me.

I dilate you with tremendous breath, I buoy you up,
Every room of the house do I fill with an arm'd force,
Lovers of me, bafflers of graves.

Sleep—I and they keep guard all night,
Not doubt, not disease shall dare to lay finger upon you,
I have embraced you, and henceforth possess you to myself,
And when you rise in the morning you will find what I tell you
        is so.

41

I am he bringing help for the sick as they pant on their backs,
And for strong upright men I bring yet more needed help.

I heard what was said of the universe,
Heard it and heard it of several thousand years;
It is middling well as far as it goes—but is that all?

Magnifying and applying come I,
Outbidding at the start the old cautious hucksters,
Taking myself the exact dimensions of Jehovah,
Lithographing Kronos, Zeus his son, and Hercules his
            grandson,
Buying drafts of Osiris, Isis, Belus, Brahma, Buddha,
In my portfolio placing Manito loose, Allah on a leaf, the
            crucifix engraved,
With Odin and the hideous-faced Mexitli and every idol and
            image,
Taking them all for what they are worth and not a cent more,
Admitting they were alive and did the work of their days,
(They bore mites as for unfledg'd birds who have now to rise
            and fly and sing for themselves.)
Accepting the rough deific sketches to fill out better in myself,
Discovering as much or more in a framer framing a house,
Putting higher claims for him there with his roll'd-up sleeves
            driving the mallet and chisel,
Not objecting to special revelations, considering a curl of smoke
            or a hair on the back of my hand just as curious as any
            revelation,
Lads ahold of fire-engines and hook-and-ladder ropes no less
            to me than the gods of the antique wars,
Minding their voices peal through the crash of destruction,
Their brawny limbs passing safe over charr'd laths, their white
            foreheads whole and unhurt out of the flames;
By the mechanic's wife with her babe at her nipple interceding
            for every person born,
Three scythes at harvest whizzing in a row from three lusty
            angels with shirts bagg'd out at their waists,

The snag-tooth'd hostler with red hair redeeming sins past and
      to come,
Selling all he possesses, traveling on foot to fee lawyers for his
      brother and sit by him while he is tried for forgery;
What was stewn in the amplest stewing the square rod about
      me, and not filling the square rod then,
The bull and the bug never worshipp'd half enough,
Dung and dirt more admirable than was dream'd,
The supernatural of no account, myself waiting my time to be
      one of the supremes,
The day getting ready for me when I shall do as much good as
      the best, and be as prodigious;
By my life-lumps! becoming already a creator,
Putting myself here and now to the ambush'd womb of the
      shadows.

A call in the midst of the crowd,
My own voice, orotund sweeping and final.

Come my children,
Come my boys and girls, my women, household and intimates,
Now the performer launches his nerve, he has pass'd his
      prelude on the reeds within.

Easily written loose-finger'd chords—I feel the thrum of your
      climax and close.

My head slues round on my neck,
Music rolls, but not from the organ,
Folks are around me, but they are no household of mine.

Ever the hard unsunk ground,
Ever the eaters and drinkers, ever the upward and downward
      sun, ever the air and the ceaseless tides,
Ever myself and my neighbors, refreshing, wicked, real,
Ever the old inexplicable query, ever that thorn'd thumb, that
      breath of itches and thirsts,
Ever the vexer's *hoot! hoot!* till we find where the sly one hides
      and bring him forth,

Ever love, ever sobbing liquid of life,
Ever the bandage under the chin, ever the trestles of death.

Here and there with dimes on the eyes walking,
To feed the greed of the belly the brains liberally spooning,
Tickets buying, taking, selling, but in to the feast never once
    going,
Many sweating, ploughing, thrashing, and then the chaff for
    payment receiving,
A few idly owning, and they the wheat continually claiming.

This is the city and I am one of the citizens,
Whatever interests the rest interests me, politics, wars, markets,
    newspapers, schools,
The mayor and councils, banks, tariffs, steamships, factories,
    stocks, stores, real estate and personal estate,

The little plentiful manikins skipping around in collars and
    tail'd coats,
I am aware who they are, (they are positively not worms or
    fleas,)
I acknowledge the duplicates of myself, the weakest and
    shallowest is deathless with me,
What I do and say the same waits for them,
Every thought that flounders in me the same flounders in
    them.

I know perfectly well my own egotism,
Know my omnivorous lines and must not write any less,
And would fetch you whoever you are flush with myself.

Not words of routine this song of mine,
But abruptly to question, to leap beyond yet nearer bring;
This printed and bound book—but the printer and the
    printing-office boy?
The well-taken photograph—but your wife or friend close and
    solid in your arms?
The black ship mail'd with iron, her mighty guns in her
    turrets—but the pluck of the captain and engineers?

In the houses the dishes and fare and furniture—but the host
    and hostess, and the look out of their eyes?
The sky up there—yet here or next door, or across the way?
The saints and sages in history—but you yourself?
Sermons, creeds, theology—but the fathomless human brain,
And what is reason? and what is love? and what is life?

43

I do not despise you priests, all time, the world over,
My faith is the greatest of faiths and the least of faiths,
Enclosing worship ancient and modern and all between ancient
    and modern,
Believing I shall come again upon the earth after five thousand
    years,
Waiting responses from oracles, honoring the gods, saluting the
    sun,
Making a fetich of the first rock or stump, powowing with
    sticks in the circle of obis,
Helping the llama or brahmin as he trims the lamps of the
    idols,
Dancing yet through the streets in a phallic procession, rapt
    and austere in the woods a gymnosophist,
Drinking mead from the skull-cup, to Shastas and Vedas
    admirant, minding the Koran,
Walking the teokallis, spotted with gore from the stone and
    knife, beating the serpent-skin drum,
Accepting the Gospels, accepting him that was crucified,
    knowing assuredly that he is divine,
To the mass kneeling or the puritan's prayer rising, or sitting
    patiently in a pew,
Ranting and frothing in my insane crisis, or waiting dead-like
    till my spirit arouses me,
Looking forth on pavement and land, or outside of pavement
    and land,
Belonging to the winders of the circuit of circuits.

One of that centripetal and centrifugal gang I turn and talk
    like a man leaving charges before a journey.

Down-hearted doubters, dull and excluded,
Frivolous, sullen, moping, angry, affected, dishearten'd
          atheistical,
I know every one of you, I know the sea of torment, doubt,
          despair and unbelief.

How the flukes splash!
How they contort rapid as lightning, with spasms and spouts of
          blood!

Be at peace bloody flukes of doubters and sullen mopers,
I take my place among you as much as among any,
This past is the push of you, me, all, precisely the same,
And what is yet untried and afterward is for you, me, all
          precisely the same.

I do not know what is untried and afterward,
But I know it will in its turn prove sufficient, and cannot fail.
Each who passes is consider'd, each who stops is consider'd, not
          a single one can it fail.

It cannot fail the young man who died and was buried,
Nor the young woman who died and was put by his side,
Nor the little child that peep'd in at the door, and then drew
          back and was never seen again,
Nor the old man who has lived without purpose, and feels it
          with bitterness worse than gall,
Nor him in the poor house tubercled by rum and the bad
          disorder,
Nor the numberless slaughter'd and wreck'd, nor the brutish
          koboo call'd the ordure of humanity ,
Nor the sacs merely floating with open mouths for food to slip
          in,
Nor any thing in the earth, or down in the oldest graves of the
          earth,
Nor any thing in the myriads of spheres, nor the myriads of
          myriads that inhabit them,
Nor the present, nor the least wisp that is known.

44

It is time to explain myself—let us stand up.

What is known I strip away,
I launch all men and women forward with me into the
        Unknown.

The clock indicates the moment—but what does eternity
        indicate?

We have thus far exhausted trillions of winters and summers,
There are trillions ahead, and trillions ahead of them.

Births have brought us richness and variety,
And other births will bring us richness and variety.
I do not call one greater and one smaller,
That which fills its period and place is equal to any.

Were mankind murderous or jealous upon you, my brother,
        my sister?
I am sorry for you, they re not murderous or jealous upon
        me,
All has been gentle with me, I keep no account with
        lamentation,
(What have I to do with lamentation?)

I am an acme of things accomplish'd, and I an encloser of
        things to be.

My feet strike an apex of the apices of the stairs,
On every step bunches of ages, and larger bunches between the
        steps,
All below duly travel'd, and still I mount and mount.

Rise after rise bow the phantoms behind me,
Afar down I see the huge first Nothing, I know I was even
        there,

I waited unseen and always, and slept through the lethargic
          mist,
And took my time, and took no hurt from the fetid carbon.

Long I was hugg'd close—long and long.

Immense have been the preparations for me,
Faithful and friendly the arms that have help'd me.

Cycles ferried my cradle, rowing and rowing like cheerful
          boatmen,
For room to me stars kept aside in their own rings,
They sent influences to look after what was to hold me.

Before I was born out of my mother generations guided me,
My embryo has never been torpid, nothing could overlay it.

For it the nebula cohered to an orb,
The long slow strata piled to rest it on,
Vast vegetables gave it sustenance,
Monstrous sauroids transported it in their mouths and
          deposited it with care.

All forces have been steadily employ'd to complete and delight
          me,
Now on this spot I stand with my robust soul!

45

O span of youth! ever-push'd elasticity.
O manhood, balanced, florid and full.

My lovers suffocate me,
Crowding my lips, thick in the pores of my skin,
Jostling me through streets and public halls, coming naked to
          me at night,
Crying by day *Ahoy!* from the rocks of the river, swinging and
          chirping over my head,
Calling my name from flower-beds, vines, tangled underbrush,

Lighting on every moment of my life,
Bussing my body with soft balsamic busses,
Noiselessly passing handfuls out of their hearts and giving
   them to be mine.

Old age superbly rising! O welcome, ineffable grace of dying
   days!
Every condition promulges not only itself, it promulges what
   grows after and out of itself,
And the dark hush promulges as much as any.

I open my scuttle at night and see the far-sprinkled systems,
And all I see multiplied as high as I can cipher edge but the
   rim of the farther systems.

Wider and wider they spread, expanding, always expanding,
Outward and outward and forever outward.

My sun has his sun and round him obediently wheels,
He joins with his partners a group of superior circuit,
And greater sets follow, making specks of the greatest inside
   them.

There is no stoppage and never can be stoppage,
If I, you, and the worlds, and all beneath or upon their
   surface, were this moment reduced back to a pallid
   float, it would not avail in the long run,
We should surely bring up again where we now stand,
And surely go as much farther, and then farther and farther.

A few quadrillions of eras, a few octillions of cubic leagues, do
   not hazard the span or make it impatient,
They are but parts, any thing is but a part.

See ever so far, there is limitless space outside of that,
Count ever so much, there is limitless time around that.

My rendezvous is appointed, it is certain,
The Lord will be there and wait till I come on perfect terms,

The great Camerado, the lover true for whom I pine will be
    there.

46

I know I have the best of time and space, and was never
    measured and never will be measured.

I tramp a perpetual journey, (come listen all!)
My signs are a rain-proof coat, good shoes, and a staff cut from
    the woods,
No friend of mine takes his ease in my chair,
I have no chair, no church, no philosophy,
I lead no man to a dinner-table, library, exchange,
But each man and each woman of you I lead upon a knoll,
My left hand hooking you round the waist,
My right hand pointing to landscapes of continents and the
    public road.

Not I not any one else can travel that road for you,
You must travel it for yourself.

It is not far, it is within reach,
Perhaps you have been on it since you were born and did not
    know,
Perhaps it is everywhere on water and on land.

Shoulder your duds dear son, and I will mine, and let us
    hasten forth,
Wonderful cities and free nations we shall fetch as we go.

If you tire, give me both burdens, and rest the chuff of your
    hand on my hip,
And in due time you shall repay the same service to me,
For after we start we never lie by again.

This day before dawn I ascended a hill and look'd at the
    crowded heaven,
And I said to my spirit *When we become the enfolders of those orbs,*

*and the pleasure and knowledge of every thing in them, shall
we be fill'd and satisfied then?*

And my spirit said *No, we but level that lift to pass and continue
beyond.*

You are also asking me questions and I hear you,
I answer that I cannot answer, you must find out for yourself.

Sit a while dear son,
Here are biscuits to eat and here is milk to drink,
But as soon as you sleep and renew yourself in sweet clothes, I
kiss you with a good-by kiss and open the gate for your
egress hence.

Long enough have you dream'd contemptible dreams,
Now I wash the gum from your eyes,
You must habit yourself to the dazzle of the light and of every
moment of your life.

Long have you timidly waded holding a plank by the shore,
Now I will you to be a bold swimmer,
To jump off in the midst of the sea, rise again, not to me,
shout, and laughingly dash with your hair.

47

I am the teacher of athletes,
He that by me speads a wider breast than my own proves the
width of my own,
He most honors my style who learns under it to destroy the
teacher.

The boy I love, the same becomes a man not through derived
power, but in his own right,
Wicked rather than virtuous out of conformity or fear,
Fond of his sweetheart, relishing well his steak,
Unrequited love or a slight cutting him worse than sharp steel
cuts,

First-rate to ride, to fight, to hit the bull's eye, to sail a skiff to
            sing a song or play on the banjo,
Preferring scars and the beard and faces pitted with small-pox
            over all latherers,
And those well-tann'd to those that keep out of the sun.

I teach straying from me, yet who can stray from me?
I follow you whoever you are from the present hour,
My words itch at your ears till you understand them.

I do not say these things for a dollar or to fill up the time while
            I wait for a boat,
(It is your talking just as much as myself, I act as the tongue of
            you,
Tied in your mouth, in mine it begins to be loosen'd.)
I swear I will never again mention love or death inside a house,
And I swear I will never translate myself at all, only to him or
            her privately stays with me in the open air.

If you would understand me go to the heights or water-shore,
The nearest gnat is an explanation, and a drop or motion of
            waves a key,
The maul, the oar, the hand-saw, second my words.

No shutter'd room or school can commune with me,
But roughs and little children better than they.

The young mechanic is closest to me, he knows me well,
The woodman that takes his axe and jug with him shall take
            me with him all day,
The farm-boy ploughing in the field feels good at the sound of
            my voice,
In vessels that sail my words sail, I go with fishermen and
            seamen and love them.

The soldier camp'd or upon the march is mine,
On the night ere the pending battle many seek me, and I do not
            fail them,

On that solemn night (it may be their last) those that know me
      seek me.

My face rubs to the hunter's face when he lies down alone in
      his blanket,
The driver thinking of me does not mind the holt of his wagon,
The young mother and old mother comprehend me,
The girl and the wife rest the needle a moment and forget
      where they are,
They and all would resume what I have told them.

48

I have said that the soul is not more than the body,
And I have said that the body is not more than the soul,
And nothing, not God, is greater to one than one's self is,
And whoever walks a furlong without sympathy walks to his
      own funeral drest in his shroud,
And I or you pocketless of a dime may purchase the pick of
      the earth,
And to glance with an eye or show a bean in its pod confounds
      the learning of all times,
And there is no trade or employment but the young man
      following it may become a hero,
And there is no object so soft but it makes a hub for the
      wheel'd universe,
And I say to any man or woman, Let your soul stand cool and
      composed before a million universes.

And I say to mankind, Be not curious about God,
For I who am curious about each am not curious about God,
(No array of terms can say how much I am at peace about God
      and about death.)

I hear and behold God in every object, yet understand God not
      in the least,
Nor do I understand who there can be more wonderful than
      myself.

Why should I wish to see God better than this day?
I see something of God each hour of the twenty-four, and each
  moment then,
In the faces of men and women I see God, and in my own face
  in the glass,
I find letters from God dropt in the street, and every one is
  sign'd by God's name,
And I leave them where they are, for I know that wheresoe'er
  I go
Others will punctually come for ever and ever.

49

And as to you Death, and you bitter hug of mortality, it is idle
  to try to alarm me.
To his work without flinching the accoucheur comes,
I see the elder-hand pressing receiving supporting,
I recline by the sills of the exquisite flexible doors,
And mark the outlet, and mark the relief and escape.

And as to you Corpse I think you are good manure, but that
  does not offend me,
I smell the white roses sweet-scented and growing,
I reach to the leafy lips, I reach to the polish'd breasts of
  melons.

And as you Life I reckon you are the leavings of many
  deaths,
(No doubt I have died myself ten thousand times before.)

I hear you whispering there O stars in heaven,
O suns—O grass of graves—O perpetual transfers and
  promotions,
If you do not say any thing how can I say any thing?

Of the turbid pool that lies in the autumn forest,
Of the moon that descends the steeps of the soughing twilight,
Toss, sparkles of day and dusk—toss on the black stems that
  decay in the muck.

Toss to the moaning gibberish of the dry limbs.

I ascend from the moon, I ascend from the night,
I perceive that the ghastly glimmer is noonday sunbeams
    reflected,
And debouch to the steady and central from the offspring
    great or small.

50

There is that in me—I do not know what it is—but I know it is
    in me.

Wrench'd and sweaty—calm and cool then my body becomes,
I sleep—I sleep long.

I do not know it—it is without name—it is a word unsaid,
It is not in any dictionary, utterance, symbol.

Something it swings on more than the earth I swing on,
To it the creation is the friend whose embracing awakes me.

Perhaps I might tell more. Outlines! I plead for my brothers
    and sisters.

Do you see O my brothers and sisters?
It is not chaos or death—it is form, union, plan—it is eternal
    life—it is Happiness.

51

The past and present wilt—I have fill'd them, emptied them,
And proceed to fill my next fold of the future.

Listener up there! what have you to confide to me?
Look in my face while I snuff the sidle of evening,
(Talk honestly, no one else hears you, and I stay only a minute
    longer.)

Do I contradict myself?
Very well then I contradict myself,
(I am large, I contain multitudes.)

I concentrate toward them that are nigh, I wait on the
          door-slab.

Who has done his day's work? who will soonest be through with
          his supper?
Who wishes to walk with me?

Will you speak before I am gone? will you prove already too
          late?

The spotted hawk swoops by and accuses me, he complains of
          my gab and my loitering.

I too am not a bit tamed, I too am untranslatable,
I sound my barbaric yawp over the roofs of the world.

The last scud of day holds back for me,
It flings my likeness after the rest and true as any on the
          shadow'd wilds,
It coaxes me to the vapor and the dusk.

I depart as air, I shake my white locks at the runaway sun,
I effuse my flesh in eddies, and drift it in lacy jags.

I bequeath myself to the dirt to grow from the grass I love,
If you want me again look for me under your boot-soles.

You will hardly know who I am or what I mean,
But I shall be good health to you nevertheless,
And filter and fibre your blood.

Failing to fetch me at first keep encouraged,
Missing me one place search another,
I stop somewhere waiting for you.

The Sleepers [1855]

1

I wander all night in my vision,
Stepping with light feet, swiftly and noiselessly stepping and
    stopping,
Bending with open eyes over the shut eyes of sleepers,
Wandering and confused, lost to myself, ill-assorted,
contradictory,
Pausing, gazing, bending, and stopping,

How solemn they look there, stretch'd and still,
How quiet they breathe, the little children in their cradles.

The wretched features of ennuyés, the white features of
    corpses, the livid faces of drunkards, the sick-gray faces
    of onanists,
The gash'd bodies on battle-fields, the insane in their
    strong-door'd rooms, the sacred idiots, the new-born
    emerging from gates, and the dying emerging from
    gates,
The night pervades them and infolds them.

The married couple sleep calmly in their bed, he with his
    palm on the hip of the wife, and she with her palm on
    the hip of the husband,
The sisters sleep lovingly side by side in their bed,
The men sleep lovingly side by side in theirs
And the mother sleeps with her little child carefully wrapt.

The blind sleep, and the deaf and dumb sleep,
The prisoner sleeps well in the prison, the runaway son
    sleeps,
The murderer that is to be hung the next day, how does he
    sleep?
And the murder'd person, how does he sleep?

The female that loves unrequited sleeps,
And the male that loves unrequited sleeps,
The head of the money-maker that plotted all day sleeps,
And the enraged and treacherous dispositions, all, all sleep.

I stand in the dark with drooping eyes by the worst-suffering
          and the most restless,
I pass my hands soothingly to and fro a few inches from
          them,
The restless sink in their beds, they fitfully sleep.

Now I pierce the darkness, new beings appear,
The earth recedes from me into the night,
I saw that it was beautiful, and I see that what is not the earth
          is beautiful.
I go from bedside to bedside, I sleep close with the other
          sleepers each in turn,
I dream in my dream all the dreams of the other dreamers,
And I become the other dreamers.

I am a dance—play up there! the fit is whirling me fast!

I am the ever-laughing—it is new moon and twilight,
I see the hiding of douceurs, I see nimble ghosts whichever
          way I look,
Cache and cache again deep in the ground and sea, and
          where is it neither ground nor sea.

Well do they do their jobs those journeymen divine,
Only from me can they hide nothing, and would not if they
          could,

I reckon I am their boss and they make me a pet besides,
And surround me and lead me and run ahead when I walk,
To lift their cunning covers to signify me with stretch'd arms,
          and resume the way;
Onward we move, a gay gang of blackguards! with
          mirth-shouting music and wild-flapping pennants of joy!

I am the actor, the actress, the voter, the politician,
The emigrant and the exile, the criminal that stood in the
        box,
He who has been famous and he who shall be famous after
        to-day,
The stammerer, the well-formed person, the wasted or feeble
        person.

I am she who adorn'd herself and folded her hair expectantly,
My truant lover has come, and it is dark.

Double yourself and receive me darkness,
Receive me and my lover too, he will not let me go without
        him.

I roll myself upon you as upon a bed, I resign myself to the
        dusk.

He whom I call answers me and takes the place of my lover,
He rises with me silently from the bed.

Darkness, you are gentler than my lover, his flesh was sweaty
        and panting,
I feel the hot moisture yet that he left me.

My hands are spread forth, I pass them in all directions,
I would sound up the shadowy shore so which you are
        journeying.

Be careful darkness! already what was it touch'd me?
I thought my lover had gone, else darkness and he are one,
I hear the heart-beat, I follow, I fade away.

2

I desend my western course, my sinews are flaccid,
Perfume and youth course through me and I am their wake.

It is my face yellow and wrinkled instead of the old woman's,

I sit low in a straw-bottom chair and carefully darn my
    grandson's stockings.

It is I too, the sleepless widow looking out on the winter
    midnight,
I see the sparkles of starshine on the icy and pallid earth.

A shroud I see and I am the shroud, I wrap a body and lie in
    the coffin,
It is dark here under ground, it is not evil or pain here, it is
    blank here, for reasons.

(It seems to me that every thing in the light and air ought to
    be happy,
Whoever is not in his coffin and the dark grave let him know
    he has enough.)

3

I see a beautiful gigantic swimmer swimming naked through
    the eddies of the sea,
His brown hair lies close and even to his head, he strikes out
    with courageous arms, he urges himself with his legs,

I see his white body, I see his undaunted eyes,
I hate the swift-running eddies that would dash him
    head-foremost on the rocks.

What are you doing you ruffianly red-trickled waves?
Will you kill the courageous giant? will you kill him in the
    prime of his middle age?

Steady and long he struggles,
He is baffled, bang'd, bruis'd, he holds out while his strength
    holds out,
The slapping eddies are spotted with his blood, they bear him
    away, they roll him, swing him, turn him,
His beautiful body is borne in the circling eddies, it is
    continually bruis'd on rocks,

Swiftly and out of sight is borne the brave corpse.

4

I turn but do not extricate myself,
Confused, a past-reading, another, but with darkness yet.

The beach is cut by the razory ice-wind, the wreck-guns
        sound,
The tempest lulls, the moon comes floundering through the
        drifts.
I look where the ship helplessly heads end on, I hear the
        burst as she strikes, I hear the howls of dismay, they
        grow fainter and fainter.

I cannot aid with my wringing fingers,
I can but rush to the surf and let it drench me and freeze upon
        me.

I search with the crowd, not one of the company is wash'd to
        us alive,
In the morning I help pick up the dead and lay them in rows
        in a barn.

5

Now of the older war-days, the defeat at Brooklyn,
Washington stands inside the lines, he stands on the intrench'd
        hills amid a crowd of officers,
His face is cold and damp, he cannot repress the weeping
        drops,
He lifts the glass perpetually to his eyes, the color is blanch'd
        from his cheeks,
He sees the slaughter of the southern braves confided to him
        by their parents.

The same at last and at last when peace is declared,
He stands in the room of the old tavern, the well-belov'd
        soldiers all pass through,

The officers speechless and slow draw near in their turns,
The chief encircles their necks with his arm and kisses them on
        the cheek,
He kisses lightly the wet cheeks one after another, he shakes
        hands and bids good-by to the army.

6

Now what my mother told me one day as we sat at dinner
        together,
Of when she was a nearly grown girl living home with her
        parents on the old homestead.

A red squaw came one breakfast-time to the old homestead,
On her back she carried a bundle of rushes for rush-bottoming
        chairs,
Her hair, straight, shiny, coarse, black, profuse, half-envelop'd
        her face,
Her step was free and elastic, and her voice sounded
        exquisitely as she spoke.

My mother look'd in delight and amazement at the stranger,
She look'd at the freshness of her tall-borne face and full and
        pliant limbs,
The more she look'd upon her she loved her,
Never before had she seen such a wonderful beauty and purity,
She made her sit on a bench by the jamb of the fireplace, she
        cook'd food for her,
She had no work to give her, but she gave her remembrance
        and fondness.

The red squaw staid all the forenoon, and toward the middle
        of the afternoon she went away,
O my mother was loth to have her go away,
All the week she thought of her, she watch'd for her many a
        month,
She remember'd her many a winter and many a summer,
But the red squaw never came nor was heard of there again.

7

A show of the summer softness—a contact of something
        unseen—an amour of the light and air,
I am jealous and overwhelm'd with friendliness,
And will go gallivant with the light and air myself.

O love and summer, you are in the dreams and in me,
Autumn and winter are in the dreams, the farmer goes with his
        thrift,
The droves and crops increase, the barns are well-fill'd.

Elements merge in the night, ships make tacks in the dreams,
The sailor sails, the exile returns home,
The fugitive returns unharm'd, the immigrant is back beyond
        months and years,
The poor Irishman lives in the simple house of his childhood
        with the well-known neighbors and faces,
They warmly welcome him, he is barefoot again, he forgets he
        is well off,
The Dutchman voyages home, and the Scotchman and
        Welshman voyage home, and the native of the
        Mediterranean voyages home,
To every port of England, France, Spain, enter well-fill'd ships,
The Swiss foots it toward his hills, the Prussian goes his way,
        the Hungarian his way, and the Pole his way,
The Swede returns, and the Dane and Norwegian return.

The homeward bound and the outward bound,
The beautiful lost swimmer, the ennuyé, the onanist, the
        female that loves unrequited, the money-maker,
The actor and actress, those through with their parts and those
        waiting to commence,
The affectionate boy, the husband and wife, the voter, the
        nominee that is chosen and the nominee that has fail'd,
The great already known and the great any time after to-day,
The stammerer, the sick, the perfect-form'd, the homely,
The criminal that stood in the box, the judge that sat and

sentenced him, the fluent lawyers, the jury, the audience,
The laughter and weeper, the dancer, the midnight widow, the
     red squaw,
The consumptive, the erysipalite, the idiot, he that is wrong'd.
The antipodes, and every one between this and them in the
     dark,
I swear they are averaged now—one is no better than the
     other,
The night and sleep have liken'd them and restored them.
I swear they are all beautiful,
Every one that sleeps is beautiful, every thing in the dim light
     is beautiful,
The wildest and bloodiest is over, and all is peace.

Peace is always beautiful,
The myth of heaven indicates peace and night.

The myth of heaven indicates the soul,
The soul is always beautiful, it appears more or it appears less,
     it comes or it lags behind,
It comes from its embower'd garden and looks pleasantly on
     itself and encloses the world,
Perfect and clean the genitals previously jetting, and perfect
     and clean the womb cohering,
The head well-grown proportion'd and plumb, and the bowels
     and joints proportion'd and plumb.

The soul is always beautiful,
The universe is duly in order, every thing is in its place,
What has arrived is in its place and what waits shall be in its
     place,
The twisted skull waits, the watery or rotten blood waits,
The child of the glutton or venerealee waits long, and the child
     of the drunkard waits long, and the drunkard himself
     waits long,
The sleepers that lived and died wait, the far advanced are to
     go on in their turns, and the far behind are to come on
     in their turns,

The diverse shall be no less diverse, but they shall flow and
    unite—they unite now.

8

The sleepers are very beautiful as they lie unclothed,
They flow hand in hand over the whole earth from east to west
    as they lie unclothed,
The Asiatic and African are hand in hand, the European and
    American are hand in hand,
Learn'd and unlearn'd are hand in hand, and male and female
    are hand in hand,
The bare arm of the girl crosses the bare breast of her lover,
    they press close without lust, his lips press her neck,
The father holds his grown or ungrown son in his arms with
    measureless love, and the son holds the father in his
    arms with measureless love,
The white hair of the mother shines on the white wrist of the
    daughter,
The breath of the boy goes with the breath of the man, friend
    is inarm'd by friend,
The scholar kisses the teacher and the teacher kisses the
    scholar, the wrong'd is made right,
The call of the slave is one with the master's call, and the
    master salutes the slave,
The felon steps forth from the prison, the insane becomes
    sane, the suffering of sick persons is reliev'd,
The sweatings and fevers stop, the throat that was unsound is
    sound, the lungs of the consumptive are resumed, the
    poor distress'd head is free,
The joints of the rheumatic move as smoothly as ever, and
    smoother than ever,
Stiflings and passages open, the paralyzed become supple,
The swell'd and convuls'd and congested awake to themselves
    in condition,
They pass the invigoration of the night and the chemistry of
    the night, and awake.

I too pass from the night,

I stay a while away O night, but I return to you again and love
    you.

Why should I be afraid to trust myself to you?
I am not afraid, I have been well brought forward by you,
I love the rich running day but I do not desert her in whom I
    lay so long,
I know not how I came of you and I know not where I go with
    you, but I know I came well and shall go well.

I will stop only a time with the night, and rise betimes,
I will duly pass the day O my mother, and duly return to you.

When Lilacs Last in the Dooryard Bloom'd [1865-66]

1

When lilacs last in the dooryard bloom'd,
And the great star early droop'd in the western sky in the
    night,
I mourn'd, and yet shall mourn with ever-returning spring,

Ever-returning spring, trinity sure to me you bring,
Lilac blooming perennial and drooping star in the west,
And thought of him I love.

2

O powerful western fallen star!
O shades of night—O moody, tearful night!
O great star disappear'd—O the black murk that hides
    the star!
O cruel hands that hold me powerless—O helpless soul
    of me!
O harsh surrounding cloud that will not free my soul.

3

In the dooryard fronting an old farm-house near the
    white-wash'd palings,
Stands the lilac-bush tall-growing with heart-shaped leaves
    of rich green,
With many a pointed blossom rising delicate, with the
    perfume strong I love,
With every leaf a miracle—and from this bush in the
    dooryard,
With delicate-color'd blossoms and heart-shaped leaves of
    rich green,
A sprig with its flower I break.

4

In the swamp in secluded recesses,
A shy and hidden bird is warbling a song.

Solitary the thrush,
The hermit withdrawn to himself, avoiding the settlements,
Sings by himself a song.

Song of the bleeding throat,
Death's outlet song of life, (for well dear brother I know,
If thou wast not granted to sing thou would'st surely die.)

5

Over the breast of the spring, the land, amid cities,
Amid lanes and through old woods, where lately the violets
    peep'd from the ground, spotting the gray debris,
Amid the grass in the fields each side of the lanes, passing
    the endless grass,
Passing the yellow-spear'd wheat, every grain from its
    shroud in the dark-brown fields uprisen,
Passing the apple-tree blows of white and pink in the
    orchards,
Carrying a corpse to where it shall rest in the grave,
Night and day journeys a coffin.

6

Coffin that passes through lanes and streets,
Through day and night with the great cloud darkening
        the land,
With the pomp of the inloop'd flags with the cities draped
        in black,
With the show of the States themselves as of carpe-veil'd
        women standing,
With processions long and winding and the flambeaus
        of the night,
With the countless torches lit, with the silent sea of faces
        and the unbared heads,
With the waiting depot, the arriving coffin, and the sombre
        faces,
With dirges through the night, with the thousand voices
        rising strong and solemn,
With all the mournful voices of the dirges pour'd around
        the coffin,
The dim-lit churches and the shuddering organs—where
        amid these you journey,
With the tolling tolling bells' perpetual clang,
Here, coffin that slowly passes,
I give you my sprig of lilac.

7

(Nor for you, for one alone,
Blossoms and branches green to coffins all I bring,
For fresh as the morning, thus would I chant a song for you
        O sane and sacred death.

All over bouquets of roses,
O death, I cover you over with roses and early lilies,
But mostly and now the lilac that blooms the first,
Copious I break, I break the sprigs from the bushes,
With loaded arms I come, pouring for you,
For you and the coffins all of you O death.)

8

O western orb sailing the heaven,
Now I know what you must have meant as a month since I
    walk'd,
As I walk'd in silence the transparent shadowy night,
As I saw you had something to tell as you bent to me night
    after night,
As you droop'd from the sky low down as if to my side,
    (while the other stars all look'd on,)
As we wander'd together the solemn night, (for something
    I know not what kept me from sleep,)
As the night advanced, and I saw on the rim of the west
    how full you were of woe,
As I stood on the rising ground in the breeze in the cool
    transparent night,
As I watch'd where you pass'd and was lost in the
    netherward black of the night,
As my soul in its trouble dissatisfied sank, as where you
    sad orb,
Concluded, dropt in the night, and was gone.

9

Sing on there in the swamp,
O singer bashful and tender, I hear your notes, I hear
    your call,
I hear, I come presently, I understand you,
But a moment I linger, for the lustrous star has detain'd me,
The star my departing comrade holds and detains me.

10

O how shall I warble myself for the dead one there I loved?
And how shall I deck my song for the large sweet soul
    that has gone?
And what shall my perfume be for the grave of him I love?

Sea-winds blown from east and west,

Blown from the Eastern sea and blown from the Western
       sea, till there on the prairies meeting,
These and with these and the breath of my chant,
I'll perfume the grave of him I love.

11

O what shall I hang on the chamber walls?
And what shall the pictures be that I hang on the walls,
To adorn the burial-house of him I love?

Pictures of growing spring and farms and homes,
With the Fourth-month eve at sundown, and the gray
       smoke lucid and bright,
With floods of the yellow gold of the gorgeous, indolent,
       sinking sun, burning, expanding the air,
With the fresh sweet herbage under foot, and the pale green
       leaves of the trees prolific,
In the distance the flowing glaze, the breast of the river,
       with a wind-dapple here and there,
With ranging hills on the banks, with many a line against
       the sky, and shadows,
And the city at hand with dwellings so dense, and stacks of
       chimneys,
And all the scenes of life and the workshops, and the
       workmen homeward returning.

12

Lo, body and soul—this land,
My own Manhattan with spires, and the sparkling and
       hurrying tides, and the ships,
The varied and ample land, the South and the North in the
       light, Ohio's shores and flashing Missouri,
And ever the far-spreading prairies cover'd with grass
       and corn.

Lo, the most excellent sun so calm and haughty,
The violet and purple morn with just-felt breezes,

The gentle soft-born measureless light,
The miracle spreading bathing all, the fulfill'd noon,
The coming eve delicious, the welcome night and the stars,
Over my cities shining all, enveloping man and land.

13

Sing on, sing on you gray-brown bird,
Sing from the swamps, the recesses, pour your chant from
    the bushes,
Limitless out of the dusk, out of the cedars and pines.

Sing on dearest brother, warble your reedy song,
Loud human song, with voice of uttermost woe,

O liquid and free and tender!
O wild and loose to my soul—O wondrous singer!
You only I hear—yet the star holds me, (but will soon
    depart,)
Yet the lilac with mastering odor holds me.

14

Now while I sat in the day and look'd forth,
In the close of the day with its light and the fields of spring,
    and the farmers preparing their crops,
In the large unconscious scenery of my land with its lakes
    and forests,
In the heavenly aerial beauty, (after the perturb'd winds
    and the storms,)

Under the arching heavens of the afternoon swift passing,
    and the voices of children and women,
The many-moving sea-tides, and I saw the ships how they
    sail'd,
And the summer approaching with richness, and the fields
    all busy with labor,
And the infinite separate houses, how they all went on,
    each with its meals and minutia of daily usages,

And the streets how their throbbings throbb'd, and the
      cities pent—lo, then and there,
Falling upon them all and among them all, enveloping me
      with the rest,
Appear'd the cloud, appear'd the long black trail,
And I knew death, its thought, and the sacred knowledge
      of death.

Then with the knowledge of death as walking one side of me,
And the thought of death close-walking the other side of me,
And I in the middle as with companions, and as holding
      the hands of companions,
I fled forth to the hiding receiving night that talks not,
Down to the shores of the water, the path by the swamp
      in the dimness,
To the solemn shadowy cedars and ghostly pines so still.

And the singer so shy to the rest receiv'd me,
The gray-brown bird I know receiv'd us comrades three,
And he sang the carol of death, and a verse for him I love.

From deep secluded recesses,
From the fragrant cedars and the ghostly pines so still,
Came the carol of the bird.

And the charm of the carol rapt me,
As I held as if by their hands my comrades in the night,
And the voice of my spirit tallied the song of the bird.

Come lovely and soothing death,
Undulate round the world, serenely arriving, arriving,
In the day, in the night, to all, to each,
Sooner or later delicate death.

Prais'd be the fathomless universe,
For life and joy, and for objects and knowledge curious,
And for love, sweet love—but praise! praise! praise!
For the sure-enwinding arms of cool-enfolding death.

Dark mother always gliding near with soft feet,
Have none chanted for thee a chant of fullest welcome?
Then I chant it for thee, I glorify thee above all,
I bring thee a song that when thou must indeed come,
come unfalteringly.

Approach strong deliveress,
When it is so, when thou hast taken them I joyously sing
the dead,
Lost in the loving floating ocean of thee,
Laved in the flood of thy bliss O death.

From me to thee glad serenades,
Dances for thee I propose saluting thee, adornments and
feastings for thee,
And the sights of the open landscape and the high-spread
sky are fitting,
And life and the fields, and the huge and thoughtful night.

The night in silence under many a star,
The ocean shore and the husky whispering wave whose
voice I know,
And the soul turning to thee O vast and well-veil'd death,
And the body gratefully nestling close to thee.

Over the tree-tops I float thee a song,
Over the rising and sinking waves, over the myriad fields
and the prairies wide,
Over the dense-pack'd cities all and the teeming wharves
and ways,
I float this carol with joy, with joy to thee O death.

15

To the tally of my soul,
Loud and strong kept up the gray-brown bird,
With pure deliberate notes spreading filling the night.

Loud in the pines and cedars dim,

Clear in the freshness moist and the swamp-perfume,
And I with my comrades there in the night.

While my sight that was bound in my eyes unclosed,
As to long panoramas of visions.

And I saw askant the armies,
I saw as in noiseless dreams hundreds of battle-flags,
Borne through the smoke of the battles and pierc'd with
          missiles I saw them,
And carried hither and you through the smoke, and torn
          and bloody,
And at last but a few shreds left on the staffs, (and all in
          silence,)
And the staffs all splinter'd and broken.

I saw battle-corpses, myriads of them,
And the white skeletons of young men, I saw them,
I saw the debris and debris of all the slain soldiers of the war,
But I saw they were not as was thought,
They themselves were fully at rest, they suffer'd not,
The living remain'd and suffer'd, the mother suffer'd,
And the wife and the child and the musing comrade suffer'd,
And the armies that remain'd suffer'd.

16

Passing the visions, passing the night,
Passing, unloosing the hold of my comrades' hands,
Passing the song of the hermit bird and the tallying song
          of my soul,
Victorious song, death's outlet song, yet varying
          ever-altering song,
As low and wailing, yet clear the notes, rising and falling,
          flooding the night,
Sadly sinking and fainting, as warning and warning, and
          yet again bursting with joy,
Covering the earth and filling the spread of the heaven,
As that powerful psalm in the night I heard from recesses,

Passing, I leave thee lilac with heart-shaped leaves,
I leave thee there in the door-yard, blooming, returning
　　with spring.

I cease from my song for thee,
From my gaze on thee in the west, fronting the west,
　　communing with thee,
O comrade lustrous with silver face in the night.

Yet each to keep and all, retrievements out of the night,
The song, the wondrous chant of the gray-brown bird,
And the tallying chant, the echo arous'd in my soul,
With the lustrous and drooping star with the countenance
　　full of woe,
With the holders holding my hand nearing the call of
　　the bird,
Comrades mine and I in the midst, and their memory ever
　　to keep, for the dead I loved so well,
For the sweetest, wisest soul of all my days and lands—and
　　this for his dear sake,
Lilac and star and bird twined with the chant of my soul,
There in the fragrant pines and the cedars dusk and dim.

HENRY TIMROD [1828-1867]

Henry Timrod was born in Charleston, South Carolina, and grew up in a home beset by financial difficulty. His mother, a widow, managed to send him to Franklin College, where he studied law and was admitted to the bar. However, he never became a successful lawyer; rather, he spent his time as a college professor and finally settled as a tutor on a South Carolina plantation. At this time, he began contributing poems to the *Southern Literary Messenger* and helped found other publications. His years of military service during the Civil War left him in a tragic condition; by the end of the war he was both ill and destitute. Nevertheless, he became famous as the War Laureate of the South. Among his major works are "The Cotton Boll," "Spring in Carolina," "Ethnogenesis," and a noble, patriotic poem, "Confederate States of America."

The Cotton Boll

While I recline
At ease beneath
This immemorial pine,
Small sphere!
(By dusky fingers brought this morning
          here
And shown with boastful smiles),
I turn thy cloven sheath,
Through which the soft white fibres peer,
That, with their gossamer bands,
Unite, like love, the sea-divided lands,
And slowly, thread by thread,
Draw forth the folded strands,
Than which the trembling line,
By whose frail help yon startled spider
          fled
Down the tall spear-grass from his swinging
          bed,

Is scarce more fine;
And as the tangled skein
Unravels in my hands,
Betwixt me and the noonday light
A veil seems lifted, and for miles and
            miles
The landscape broadens on my sight,
As, in the little boll, there lurked a spell
Like that which, in the ocean shell,
With mystic sound
Breaks down the narrow walls that hem us
            round,
And turns some city lane
Into the restless main,
With all his capes and isles !

Yonder bird,
Which floats, as if at rest,
In those blue tracts above the thunder,
            where
No vapors cloud the stainless air,
And never sound is heard,
Unless at such rare time
When, from the City of the Blest,
Rings down some golden chime,
Sees not from his high place
So vast a cirque of summer space
As widens round me in one mighty field,
Which, rimmed by seas and sands,
Doth hail its earliest daylight in the beams
Of gray Atlantic dawns;
And, broad as realms made up of many
            lands,
Is lost afar
Behind the crimson hills and purple lawns
Of sunset, among plains which roll their
            streams
Against the Evening Star !
And lo !

To the remotest point of sight,
Although I gaze upon no waste of snow,
The endless field is white;
And the whole landscape glows,
For many a shining league away,
With such accumulated light
As Polar lands would flash beneath a tropic
          day !
Nor lack there (for the vision grows,
And the small charm within my hands—
More potent even than the fabled one,
Which oped whatever golden mystery
Lay hid in fairy wood or magic vale,
T he curious ointment of the Arabian tale—
Beyond all mortal sense
Doth stretch my sight's horizon, and I see,
Beneath its simple influence,
As if, with Uriel's crown,
I stood in some great temple of the Sun,
And looked, as Uriel, down !)
Nor lack there pastures rich and fields all
          green
With all the common gifts of God.
For temperate airs and torrid sheen
Weave Edens of the sod;
Through lands which look one sea of bil-
          lowy gold
Broad rivers wind their devious ways;
A hundred isles in their embraces fold
A hundred luminous bays;
And through yon purple haze
Vast mountains lift their plumëd peaks
          cloud-crowned;
And, save where up their sides the plough-
          man creeps,
An unhewn forest girds them grandly
          round,
In whose dark shades a future navy sleeps !

Ye Stars, which, though unseen, yet with
    me gaze
Upon this loveliest fragment of the earth !
Thou Sun, that kindlest all thy gentlest
    rays
Above it, as to light a favorite hearth !
Ye Clouds, that in your temples in the
    West
See nothing brighter than its humblest flow-
    ers !
And you, ye Winds, that on the ocean's
    breast
Are kissed to coolness ere ye reach its bow-
    ers !
Bear witness with me in my song of praise,
And tell the world that, since the world
    began,
No fairer land hath fired a poet's lays,
Or given a home to man.

But these are charms already widely blown !
His be the meed whose pencil's trace
Hath touched our very swamps with grace,
And round whose tuneful way
All Southern laurels bloom;
The Poet of "The Woodlands," unto whom
Alike are known
The flute's low breathing and the trumpet's
    tone,
And the soft west wind's sighs;
But who shall utter all the debt,
O Land wherein all powers are met
That bind a people's heart,
The world doth owe thee at this day,
And which it never can repay,
Yet scarcely deigns to own !
Where sleeps the poet who shall fitly sing
The source wherefrom doth spring
That mighty commerce which, confined

To the mean channels of no selfish mart,
Goes out to every shore
Of this broad earth, and throngs the sea
            with ships
That bear no thunders; hushes hungry lips
In alien lands;
Joins with a delicate web remotest strands;
And gladdening rich and poor,
Doth gild Parisian domes,
Or feed the cottage - smoke of English
            homes,
And only bounds its blessings by mankind !
In offices like these, thy mission lies,
My Country ! and it shall not end
As long as rain shall fall and Heaven bend
In blue above thee; though thy foes be
            hard
And cruel as their weapons, it shall guard
Thy hearth-stones as a bulwark; make thee
            great
In white and bloodless state;
And haply, as the years increase—
Still working through its humbler reach
With that large wisdom which the ages
            teach—
Revive the half-dead dream of universal
            peace !
As men who labor in that mine
Of Cornwall, hollowed out beneath the bed
Of ocean, when a storm rolls overhead,
Hear the dull booming of the world of
            brine
Above them, and a mighty muffled roar
Of winds and waters, yet toil calmly on,
And split the rock, and pile the massive ore,
Or carve a niche, or shape the archëd roof;
So I, as calmly, weave my woof
Of song, chanting the days to come,
Unsilenced, though the quiet summer air

Stirs with the bruit of battles, and each
        dawn
Wakes from its starry silence to the hum
Of many gathering armies. Still,
In that we sometimes hear,
Upon the Northern winds, the voice of woe
Not wholly drowned in triumph, though I
        know
The end must crown us, and a few brief
        years
Dry all our tears,
I may not sing too gladly. To Thy will
Resigned, O Lord! We cannot all forget
That there is much even Victory must re-
        gret.
And, therefore, not too long
From the great burthen of our country's
        wrong
Delay our just release!
And, if it may be, save
These sacred fields of peace
From stain of patriot or of hostile blood!
Oh, help us, Lord! to roll the crimson flood
Back on its course, and, while our banners
        wing
Northward, strike with us! till the Goth
        shall cling
To his own blasted altar-stones, and crave
Mercy; and we shall grant it, and dictate
The lenient future of his fate
There, where some rotting ships and crum-
        bling quays
Shall one day mark the Port which ruled
        the Western seas.

Quatorzain

Most men know love but as a part of life;
They hide it in some corner of the breast,
Even from themselves; and only when they
                    rest
In the brief pauses of that daily strife,
Wherewith the world might else be not so
                    rife,
They draw it forth (as one draws forth a
                    toy
To soothe some ardent, kiss-exacting boy)
And hold it up to sister, child, or wife.
Ah me! why may not love and life be one?
Why walk we thus alone, when by our side,
Love, like a visible god, might be our
                    guide?
How would the marts grow noble! and the
                    street,
Worn like a dungeon-floor by weary feet,
Seem then a golden court-way of the Sun!

Charleston [1863]

Calm as that second summer which pre-
            cedes
    The first fall of the snow,
In the broad sunlight of heroic deeds,
    The city bides the foe.

As yet, behind their ramparts, stern and
            proud.
    Her bolted thunders sleep,—
Dark Sumter, like a battlemented cloud,
    Looms o'er the solemn deep.

No Calpe frowns from lofty cliff or scaur
    To guard the holy strand;

But Moultrie holds in leash her dogs of war
    Above the level sand.

And down the dunes a thousand guns lie
        couched,
    Unseen, beside the flood,—
Like tigers in some Orient jungle crouched,
    That wait and watch for blood.

Meanwhile, through streets still echoing
        with trade,
    Walk grave and thoughtful men,
Whose hands may one day wield the pa-
        triot's blade
    As lightly as the pen.

And maidens, with such eyes as would
        grow dim
    Over a bleeding hound,
Seem each one to have caught the strength
        of him
    Whose sword she sadly bound.

Thus girt without and garrisoned at home,
    Day patient following day,
Old Charleston looks from roof and spire
        and dome,
    Across her tranquil bay.

Ships, through a hundred foes, from Saxon
        lands
    And spicy Indian ports,
Bring Saxon steel and iron to her hands,
    And summer to her courts.

But still, along yon dim Atlantic line,
    The only hostile smoke
Creeps like a harmless mist above the
        brine,

From some frail floating oak.

Shall the spring dawn, and she, still clad
        in smiles,
  And with an unscathed brow,
Rest in the strong arms of her palm-
        crowned isles,
  As fair and free as now?

We know not; in the temple of the Fates
  God has inscribed her doom:
And, all untroubled in her faith, she waits
  The triumph or the tomb.

At Magnolia Cemetery [1867]

Sleep sweetly in your humble graves,
    Sleep, martyrs of a fallen cause;
Though yet no marble column craves
    The pilgrim here to pause.

In seeds of laurel in the earth
The blossom of your fame is blown,
And somewhere, waiting for its birth,
    The shaft is in the stone !

Meanwhile, behalf the tardy years
        Which keep in trust your storied
            tombs,
Behold ! your sisters bring their tears,
    And these memorial blooms.

Small tributes ! but your shades will
            smile
        More proudly on these wreaths to-day,
Than when some cannon-moulded pile
    Shall overlook this bay.

Stoop, angels, hither from the skies !
        There is no holier spot of ground
Than where defeated valor lies,
    By mourning beauty crowned.

Ethnogenesis [1828-1867]

*Written During the Meeting of the First Southern
Congress, at Montgomery, February, 1861*

I

Hath not the morning dawned with added light?
And shall not evening call another star
Out of the infinite regions of the night,
To mark this day in Heaven? At last, we are
A nation among nations; and the world
Shall soon behold in many a distant port
            Another flag unfurled!
Now, come what may, whose favor need we court?
And, under God, whose thunder need we fear?
        Thank Him who placed us here
Beneath so kind a sky—the very sun
Takes part with us; and on our errands run
All breezes of the ocean; dew and rain
Do noiseless battle for us; and the Year,
And all the gentle daughters in her train,
March in our ranks, and in our service wield
            Long spears of golden grain!
A yellow blossom as her fairy shield,
June flings her azure banner to the wind,
    While in the order of their birth
Her sisters pass, and many an ample field
Grows white beneath their steps, till now, behold,
            Its endless sheets unfold
THE SNOW OF SOUTHERN SUMMERS! Let the earth
Rejoice! beneath those fleeces soft and warm
            Our happy land shall sleep
            In a repose as deep
    As if we lay intrenched behind
Whole leagues of Russian ice and Arctic storm!

II

And what if, mad with wrongs themselves have wrought,
      In their own treachery caught,
      By their own fears made bold,
      And leagued with him of old,
Who long since in the limits of the North
Set up his evil throne, and warred with God—
What if, both mad and blinded in their rage,
Our foes should fling us down their mortal gage,
And with a hostile step profane our sod!
We shall not shrink, my brothers, but go forth
To meet them, marshaled by the Lord of Hosts,
And overshadowed by the mighty ghosts
Of Moultrie and of Eutaw—who shall foil
Auxiliars such as these? Nor these alone,
      But every stock and stone
      Shall help us; but the very soil,
And all the generous wealth it gives to toil,
And all for which we love our noble land,
Shall fight beside, and through us; sea and strand,
      The heart of woman, and her hand,
Tree, fruit, and flower, and every influence,
      Gentle, or grave, or grand;
      The winds in our defence
Shall seem to blow; to us the hills shall lend
      Their firmness and their calm;
And in our stiffened sinews we shall blend
      The strength of pine and palm!

III

Nor would we shun the battle-ground,
      Though weak as we are strong;
Call up the clashing elements around,
      And test the right and wrong!
On one side, creeds that dare to teach
What Christ and Paul refrained to preach;
Codes built upon a broken pledge,

And Charity that whets a poniard's edge;
Fair schemes that leave the neighboring poor
To starve and shiver at the schemer's door,
While in the world's most liberal ranks enrolled,
He turns some vast philanthropy to gold;'
Religion, taking every mortal form
But that a pure and Christian faith makes warm,
Where not to vile fanatic passion urged,
Or not in vague philosophies submerged,
Repulsive with all Pharisaic leaven,
And making laws to stay the laws of Heaven!
And on the other hand, scorn of sordid gain,
Unblemished honor, truth without a stain,
Faith, justice, reverence, charitable wealth,
And, for the poor and humble, laws which give,
Not the mean right to buy the right to live,
        But life, and home, and health!
To doubt the end were want of trust in God,
        Who, if he has decreed
  That we must pass a redder sea
Than that which rang to Miriam's holy glee,
        Will surely raise at need
        A Moses with his rod!

IV

But let our fears—if fears we have—be still,
And turn us to the future! Could we climb
Some mighty Alp, and view the coming time,
    The rapturous sight would fill
        Our eyes with happy tears!
Not only for the glories which the years
Shall bring us; not for lands from sea to sea,
And wealth, and power, and peace, though these shall be;
But for the distant peoples we shall bless,
And the hushed murmurs of a world's distress:
For, to give labor to the poor,
        The whole sad planet o'er,
And save from want and crime the humblest door,

Is one among the many ends for which
       God makes us great and rich!
The hour perchance is not yet wholly ripe
When all shall own it, but the type
Whereby we shall be known in every land
Is that vast gulf which lips our Southern strand,
And through the cold, untempered ocean pours
Its genial streams, that far off Arctic shores
May sometimes catch upon the softened breeze
Strange tropic warmth and hints of summer seas.

The Unknown Dead [1873]

The rain is splashing on my sill,
But all the winds of Heaven are still;
And so it falls with that dull sound
Which thrills us in the church-yard ground,
When the first spadeful drops like lead
Upon the coffin of the dead.
Beyond my streaming window-pane,
I cannot see the neighboring vane,
Yet from its old familiar tower
The bell comes, muffled, through the shower.
What strange and unsuspected link
Of feeling touched, has made me think—
While with a vacant soul and eye
I watch that gray and stony sky—
Of nameless graves on battle-plains
Washed by a single winter's rains,
Where, some beneath Virginian hills,
And some by green Atlantic rills,
Some by the waters of the West,
A myriad unknown heroes rest.
Ah! not the chiefs, who, dying, see
Their flags in front of victory,
Or, at their life-blood's noble cost
Pay for a battle nobly lost,

Claim from their monumental beds
The bitterest tears a nation sheds.
Beneath yon lonely mound—the spot
By all save some fond few forgot—
Lie the true martyrs of the fight
Which strikes for freedom and for right.
Of them, their patriot zeal and pride,
The lofty faith that with them died,
No grateful page shall farther tell
Than that so many bravely fell;
And we can only dimly guess
What worlds of all this world's distress,
What utter woe, despair, and dearth,
Their fate has brought to many a hearth.
Just such a sky as this should weep
Above them, always, where they sleep;
Yet, haply, at this very hour,
Their graves are like a lover's bower;
And Nature's self, with eyes unwet,
Oblivious of the crimson debt
To which she owes her April grace
Laughs gayly o'er their burial-place.

The Lily Confidante [1858]

Lily, lady of the garden,
    Let me press my lip to thine:
Love must tell its story, Lily;
    Listen thou to mine.

Two I choose to know the secret—
    Thee, and yonder wordless flute:
Dragons watch me, tender Lily,
    And thou must be mute.

There's a maiden, and her name is—
    Hist! was that a rose-leaf fell?

See, the rose is listening, Lily,
    And the rose may tell.

Lily-browed and lily-hearted,
    She is very dear to me.
Lovely? yes, if being lovely
    'Is—resembling thee.

Six to half a score of summers
    Make the sweetest of the "teens"—
Not too young to guess, dear Lily,
    What a lover means.

Laughing girl and thoughtful woman,
    I am puzzled how to woo—
Shall I praise or pique her, Lily?
    Tell me what to do.

"Silly lover, if thy Lily
    Like her sister lilies be,
Thou must woo, if thou wouldst wear her,
    With a simple plea.

"Love's the lover's only magic,
    Truth the very subtlest art;
Love that feigns and lips that flatter
    Win no modest heart.

"Like the dewdrop in my bosom
    Be thy guileless language, youth:
Falsehood buyeth falsehood only;
    Truth must purchase truth.

"As thou talkest at the fireside
    With the little children by,
As thou prayest in the darkness
    When thy God is nigh,

"With a speech as chaste and gentle,

And such meanings as become
Ear of child or ear of angel,
  Speak, or be thou dumb.

"Woo her thus, and she shall give thee
  Of her heart the sinless whole,
All the girl within her bosom,
  And her woman's soul."

Spring in Carolina [1873]

Spring, with that nameless pathos in the air
Which dwells with all things fair,
Spring, with her golden suns and silver rain,
Is with us once again.

Out in the lonely woods the jasmine burns
Its fragrant lamps, and turns
Into a royal court with green festoons
The banks of dark lagoons.

In the deep heart of every forest tree
The blood is all aglee,
And there's a look about the leafless bowers
As if they dreamed of flowers.

Yet still on every side we trace the hand
Of Winter in the land,
Save where the maple reddens on the lawn,
Flushed by the season's dawn;

Or where, like those strange semblances we find
That age to childhood bind,
The elm puts on, as if in Nature's scorn,
The brown of Autumn corn.

As yet the turf is dark, although you know

That, not a span below,
A thousand germs are groping through the gloom,
And soon will burst their tomb.

Already, here and there, on frailest stems
Appear some azure gems,
Small as might deck, upon a gala day,
The forehead of a fay.

In gardens you may note amid the dearth
The crocus breaking earth;
And near the snowdrop's tender white and green,
The violet in its screen.

But many gleams and shadows need must pass
Along the budding grass,
And weeks go by, before the enamored South
Shall kiss the rose's mouth.

Still there's a sense of blossoms yet unborn
In the sweet airs of morn;
One almost looks to see the very street
Grow purple at his feet.

At times a fragrant breeze comes floating by,
And brings, you know not why,
A feeling as when eager crowds await
Before a palace gate

Some wondrous pageant; and you scarce would start,
If from a beech's heart,
A blue-eyed Dryad, stepping forth, should say,
"Behold me! I am May!"

Ah! who would couple thoughts of war and crime
With such a blessëd time!
Who in the west wind's aromatic breath
Could hear the call of Death!

Yet not more surely shall the Spring awake
The voice of wood and brake,
Than she shall rouse, for all her tranquil charms,
A million men to arms.

There shall be deeper hues upon her plains
Than all her sunlit rains,
And every gladdening influence around,
Can summon from the ground.

Oh! standing on this desecrated mould,
Methinks that I behold,
Lifting her bloody daisies up to God,
Spring kneeling on the sod,

And calling, with the voice of all her rills,
Upon the ancient hills
To fall and crush the tyrants and the slaves
Who turn her meads to graves.

SILAS WEIR MITCHELL [1829-1914]

Silas Weir Mitchell's entire life was spent in Philadelphia. He was educated at the University of Pennsylvania, but, due to poor health, he curtailed his course of study and eventually followed in the footsteps of his father, a professor of medicine at Jefferson Memorial College; he became a neurologist, famous for his successful treatment of serious nervous conditions. He was also well-known for research on rattlesnake venom. During his medical career, he became interested in creative writing and, as a result, published many anonymous poems. His prolific literary output also included prose. He is best known for "Ode on a Lycian Tomb", written in memory of his young daughter's death.

On a Boy's First Reading
of "King Henry V"

When youth was lord of my unchallenged
    fate,
And time seemed but the vassal of my will,
I entertainëd certain guests of state —
The great of older days, who, faithful still,
Have kept with me the pact my youth had
    made.

And I remember how one galleon rare
From the far distance of a time long dead
Came on the wings of a fair-fortuned air,
With sound of martial music heralded,
In blazonry of storied shields arrayed.

So the *Great Harry* with high trumpetings,
The wind of victory in her burly sails!
And all her deck with clang of armor
                    rings:
And under-flown the Lily standard trails,
And over-flown the royal Lions ramp.

The waves she rode are strewn with silent
                    wrecks,
Her proud sea-comrades once; but ever yet
Comes time - defying laughter from her
                    decks,
Where stands the lion-lord Plantagenet,
Large-hearted, merry, king of court and
                    camp.

Sail on! sail on! The fatal blasts of time
That spared so few, shall thee with joy
                    escort;

And with the stormy thunder of thy rhyme
Shalt thou salute full many a centuried port
With "Ho! for Harry and red Agin-
                    court!"

Of One Who Seemed To Have
Failed

Death's but one more to-morrow. Thou
    art gray
With many a death of many a yesterday.
O yearning heart that lacked the athlete's
    force
And, stumbling, fell upon the beaten course,
And looked, and saw with ever glazing eyes
Some lower soul that seemed to win the
    prize!
Lo, Death, the just, who comes to all alike,
Life's sorry scales of right anew shall
    strike.
Forth, through the night, on unknown
    shores to win
The peace of God unstirred by sense of sin!
There love without desire shall, like a mist
At evening precious to the drooping flower,
Possess thy soul in ownership, and kissed
By viewless lips, whose touch shall be a
    dower
Of genius and of winged serenity
Thou shalt abide in realms of poesy.
There soul hath touch of soul, and there
    the great
Cast wide to welcome thee joy's golden
    gate.
Freeborn to untold thoughts that age on age
Caressed sweet singers in their sacred
    sleep,

Thy soul shall enter on its heritage
Of God's unuttered wisdom. Thou shalt
    sweep
With hand assured the ringing lyre of life,
Till the fierce anguish of its bitter strife,
Its pain, death, discord, sorrow, and despair,

Break into rhythmic music. Thou shalt
    share
The prophet-joy that kept forever glad
God's poet-souls when alla world was sad.
Enter and live! Thou hast not lived be-
    fore;
We were but soul-cast shadows. Ah, no
    more
The heart shall bear the burdens of the
    brain;
Now shall the strong heart think, nor think
    in vain.
In the dear company of peace, and those
Who bore for man life's utmost agony,
Thy soul shall climb to cliffs of still repose,
And see before thee lie Time's mystery,
And that which is God's time, Eternity;
Whence sweeping over thee dim myriad
    things,
The awful centuries yet to be, in hosts
That stir the vast of heaven with formless
    wings,
Shall cast for thee their shrouds, and, like
    to ghosts,
Unriddle all the past, till, awed and still,
Thy soul the secret hath of good and ill.

The Quaker Graveyard

Four straight brick walls, severely plain,
    A quiet city square surround;
A level space of nameless graves,—
    The Quakers' burial-ground.

In gown of gray, or coat of drab,
    They trod the common ways of life,

With passions held in sternest leash,
    And hearts that knew not strife.

To yon grim meeting-house they fared,
    With thoughts as sober as their speech,
To voiceless prayer, to songless praise,
    To hear the elders preach.

Through quiet lengths of days they came,
    With scarce a change to this repose;
Of all life's loveliness they took
    The thorn without the rose.

But in the porch and o'er the graves,
    Glad rings the southward robin's glee,
And sparrows fill the autumn air
    With merry mutiny;

While on the graves of drab and gray
    The red and gold of autumn lie,
And wilful Nature decks the sod
    In gentlest mockery.

Idleness

There is no dearer lover of lost hours
                                    Than I.
I can be idler than the idlest flowers;
                                More idly lie
Than noonday lilies languidly afloat,
And water pillowed in a windless moat.
    And I can be
Stiller than some gray stone
That hath no motion known.
    It seems to me
That my still idleness doth make my own
    All magic gifts of joy's simplicity.

A Decanter of Madeira, Aged 86,
to George Bancroft, Aged 86, Greeting

Good Master, you and I were born
In "Teacup days" of hoop and hood,
And when the silver cue hung down,
And toasts were drunk, and wine was good;

When kin of mine (a jolly brood)
From sideboards looked, and knew full
            well
What courage they had given the beau,
How generous made the blushing belle.

Ah me! what gossip could I prate
Of days when doors were locked at din-
            ners!
Believe me, I have kissed the lips
Of many pretty saints—or sinners.

Lip service have I done, alack!
I don't repent, but come what may,
What ready lips, sir, I have kissed,
Be sure at least I shall not say.

Two honest gentlemen are we,—
I Demi John, whole George are you;
When Nature grew us one in years
She meant to make a generous brew.

She bade me store for festal hours
The sun our south-side vineyard knew;
To sterner tasks she set your life,
As statesman, writer, scholar, grew.

Years eighty-six have come and gone;
At last we meet. Your health to-night.
Take from this board of friendly hearts
The memory of a proud delight.

The days that went have made you wise,
There's wisdom in my rare bouquet.
I'm rather paler than I was;
And, on my soul, you're growing gray.

I like to think, when Toper Time
Has drained the last of me and you,
Some here shall say, They both were
       good,—
The wine we drank, the man we knew.
1886

How The Cumberland Went Down

Gray swept the angry waves
  O'er the gallant and the true,
Rolled high in mounded graves
  O'er the stately frigate's crew—
  Over cannon, over deck,
  Over all that ghastly wreck—
When the Cumberland went down.

Such a roar the waters rent
  As though a giant died,
When the wailing billows went
  Above those heroes tried;
And the sheeted foam leaped high
Like white ghosts against the sky—
  As the Cumberland went down.

O shrieking waves that gushed
  Above that loyal band,
Your cold, cold burial rushed

  O'er many a heart on land,
And from all the startled North
A cry of pain broke forth,
  When the Cumberland went down.

And forest old, that gave
  A thousand years of power
To her lordship of the wave
  And her beauty's regal dower,
Bent, as though before a blast,
When plunged her pennoned mast,
  And the Cumberland went down.

And grimy mines that sent
  To her their virgin strength,
And iron vigor lent
  To knit her lordly length
Wildly stirred with throbs of life,
Echoes of that fatal strife,
  As the Cumberland went down.

Beneath the ocean vast,
  Full many a captain bold,
By many a rotting mast,
  And admiral of old,
Rolled restless in his grave
As he felt the sobbing wave,
  When the Cumberland went down

And stern Vikings that lay
  A thousand years at rest,
In many a deep blue bay
  Beneath the Baltic's breast,
Leaped on the silver sands
And shook their rusty brands;
  As the Cumberland went down.

EMILY DICKINSON [1830-1886]

Relatively little is known of Emily Dickinson's biography. She was born in Amherst, Massachusetts, and spent most of her life as a recluse, only rarely making social appearances. As a young woman, she graduated from Amherst Academy and entered the nearby Mount Holyoke Female Seminary. Her experience in the latter institution, however, was short-lived; after a few months, she became homesick and returned to her father's house. This was a decisive step; the refuge served as the setting for her subsequent development as a prolific writer.

Nevertheless, three individuals are known to have played a significant role in her development. While still a teenager, she met Benjamin Newton, a law student who worked in her father's office. It was Newton who was primarily responsible for awakening in her an independent creative vigor. A freethinker, well-aware of the latest intellectual currents, he introduced her to new literature and especially authors such as Emerson and the Bronte sisters. His death of tuberculosis in 1853 came as a deep shock; in fact, the scholar Thomas H. Johnson believes that Dickinson first began seriously composing verse only five years after that event. This, however, is difficult to ascertain because, aside from a small number of poems from the early fifties, the poetry cannot be dated prior to 1858. Major developments in Dickinson's work from 1861-62 can be tied to the appearance of another important person. During those years, Dickinson was apparently in love with the Reverend Charles Wadsworth, a married pastor from Philadelphia. In spite of this, circumstances never allowed a lasting romance to develop because it is known that by 1862 the gentleman had parted for the West to head a congregation in San Francisco. Nevertheless, Wadsworth's impact on Dickinson appears to have been considerable, and some tentative evidence suggests that the ultimate aim of his departure was to elope. It was in 1862 that Dickinson wrote her first letter to the noted essayist and lecturer Thomas Higginson who had come to her attention as the author of an article in an issue of the *Atlantic Monthly*. In this article, Higginson offered inspiring ideas and advice to young writers. For Dickinson this proved to be a timely opportunity; being unsure of her abilities, she decided to obtain professional evaluation of a growing collection of poems. Unfortunately, Higginson's initial reaction was cautious; he felt that the work lacked polish and was too eccentric for publication. He did, however, show a marked interest in Dickinson's qualities as a person. Thus, he eventually became a close friend and a source of inspiration in the future.

Although the early to mid-sixties were Dickinson's most prolific years, some of her finest works belong to a later period. It is curious that, throughout her career, she resisted publication; this seemed to stem from a firm decision to maintain a private style of life and to protect her creative output from criticism. Moreover, Dickinson had understood that dealing with publishers could be likened to "an auction of the soul" and that editors could be ruthless; her experience showed that many did not understand the pecularities of style and preferred to see it conform to accepted procedures in the use of rhyme and metaphor. As a result, she contented herself by writing for personal pleasure and for a few, select friends with whom she maintained contact through correspondence.

In 1858, Dickinson began the practice of assembling short poems into groups: she would copy them on letter paper and sew the sheets together with needle and thread. Each packet containing as many as a half dozen sheets was arranged thematically. All in all, she left approximately sixty such packets. Most of her poetry, however, was not brought to light until after her death in 1886. Her sister found well over one thousand poems on carefully printed manuscripts and gave them to the editor, Mabel Loomis Todd, who, in turn, summoned Thomas Higginson to prepare them for publication. *Poems,* a selection of one hundred and fifteen verses, was published, in November, 1890. Although the volume did not receive favorable reviews, there were repeated popular demands for new printings. Encouraged by this success, Todd assembled two volumes of letters by the poet in 1894 and, finally, more poems in 1896.

Hope Is the Thing with Feathers

Hope is the thing with feathers
That perches in the soul,
And sings the tune without the words,
And never stops at all,

And sweetest in the gale is heard;
And sore must be the storm
That could abash the little bird
That kept so many warm.

I've heard it in the chillest land,
And on the strangest sea;
Yet, never, in extremity,
It asked a crumb of me.

If Anybody's Friend Be Dead

If anybody's friend be dead,
It's sharpest of the theme

Their costume, of a Sunday,
Some manner of the hair,—
A prank nobody knew but them,
Lost, in the sepulchre.

How warm they were on such a day:
You almost feel the date,
So short way off it seems; and now,
They're centuries from that.

How pleased they were at what you
        said;
You try to touch the smile,
The thinking how they walked alive,
At such and such a time.

And dip your fingers in the frost:
When was it, can you tell,

You asked the company to tea,
Acquaintance, just a few,
And chatted close with this grand thing
That don't remember you?

Past bows and invitations,
Past interview, and vow,
Past what ourselves can estimate,—
That makes the quick of woe!

I Years Had Been From Here

I Years had been from Home
And now before the Door
I dared not enter, lest a Face
I never saw before

Stare stolid into mine
And ask my Business there—
"My Business but a Life I left
Was such remaining there?"

I leaned upon the Awe—
I lingered with Before—
The Second like an Ocean rolled
And broke against my ear—

I laughed a crumbling Laugh
That I could fear a Door
Who Consternation compassed
And never winced before.

I fitted to the Latch
My Hand, with trembling care
Lest back the awful Door should spring
And leave me in the Floor—

Then moved my Fingers off
As cautiously as Glass
And held my ears, and like a Thief
Fled gasping from the House—

Faith is a Fine Invention

"Faith" is a fine invention
When Gentlemen can *see*—
But *Microscopes* are prudent
In an Emergency.

The Last Night That She Lived

The last Night that She lived
It was a Common Night
Except the Dying—this to Us
Made Nature different

We noticed smallest things—
Things overlooked before
By this great light upon our Minds
Italicized—as 'twere.

As We went out and in
Between Her final Room
And Rooms where Those to be alive
Tomorrow were, a Blame

That Others could exist
While She must finish quite
A jealousy for Her arose
So nearly infinite—

We waited while She passed—
It was a narrow time—
Too jostled were Our Souls to speak
At length the notice came.

She mentioned, and forgot—
Then lightly as a Reed
Bent to the Water, struggled scarce—
Consented, and was dead—

And We—We placed the Hair—
And drew the Head erect—
And then an awful leisure was
Belief to regulate—

The Heart Asks For Pleasure First

The Heart asks Pleasure—first—
And then—Excuse from Pain—

And then—those little Anodynes
That deaden suffering—

And then—to go to sleep—
And then—if it should be
The will of its Inquisitor
The privilege to die—

This Quiet Dust Was Gentlemen and Ladies

This quiet Dust was Gentlemen and Ladies
And Lads and Girls—
Was laughter and ability and Sighing
And Frocks and Curls.

This Passive Place a Summer's nimble mansion
Where Bloom and Bees
Exists an Oriental Circuit
Then cease, like these—

Unto My Books So Good to Turn

Unto my Books—so good to turn—
Far ends of tired Days—
It half endears the Abstinence—
And Pain—is missed—in Praise—

As Flavors—cheer Retarded Guests
With Banquettings to be—
So Spices—stimulate the time
Till my small Library—

It may be Wilderness—without—
Far feet of failing Men—
But Holiday—excludes the night—
And it is Bells—within—

I thank these Kinsmen of the Shelf—
Their Countenances Kid
Enamor—in Prospective—
And satisfy—obtained—

I'll Tell You How The Sun Rose

I'll tell you how the Sun rose—
A Ribbon at a time—
The Steeples swam in Amethyst—
The news, like Squirrels, ran—

The Hills untied their Bonnets—
The Bobolinks—begun—
Then I said softly to myself—
"That must have been the Sun"!
But how he set—I know not—
There seemed a purple stile
That little Yellow boys and girls
Were climbing all the while—
Till when they reached the other side,
A Dominie in Gray—
Put gently up the evening Bars—
And led the flock away—

Fame of Myself to Justify

Fame of Myself, to justify,
All other Plaudit be
Superfluous—An Incense
Beyond Necessity—

Fame of Myself to lack—Although
My Name be else Supreme—
This were an Honor honorless—
A futile Diadem—

The Sky is Low, The Clouds Are Mean

The Sky is low—the Clouds are mean.
A Travelling Flake of Snow
Across a Barn or through a Rut
Debates if it will go—

A Narrow Wind complains all Day
How some one treated him

Nature, like Us is sometimes caught
Without her Diadem.

I Know Some Lonely Houses off the Road

I know some lonely Houses off the Road
A Robber'd like the look of—
Wooden barred,
And Windows hanging low,
Inviting to—
A Portico,
Where two could creep—
One—hand the Tools—
The other peep—
To make sure All's Asleep—
Old fashioned eyes—
Not easy to surprise!

How orderly the Kitchen'd look, by night,
With just a Clock—
But they could gag the Tick—
And Mice won't bark—
And so the Walls—don't tell—
None—will—

A pair of Spectacles ajar just stir—
An Almanac's aware—
Was it the Mat—winked,
Or a Nervous Star?
The Moon—slides down the stair,
To see who's there!

There's plunder—where—
Tankard, or Spoon—

Earring—or Stone—
A Watch—Some Ancient Brooch
To match the Grandmama—
Staid sleeping—there—

Day—rattles—too
Stealth's—slow—

The Sun has got as far
As the third Sycamore—
Screams Chanticleer
"Who's there"?

And Echoes—Trains away,
Sneer—"Where"!
While the old Couple, just astir,
Fancy the Sunrise—left the door ajar!

The Brain Is Wider Than the Sky

The Brain—is wider than the Sky—
For—put them side by side—
The one the other will contain
With ease—and You—beside—

The Brain is deeper than the sea—
For—hold them—Blue to Blue—
The one the other will absorb—
As Sponges—Buckets—do—

The Brain is just the weight of God—
For—Heft them—Pound for Pound—
And they will differ—if they do—
As Syllable from Sound—

Glory is That Bright Tragic Thing

Glory is that bright tragic thing
That for an instant
Means Dominion—
Warms some poor name
That never felt the Sun,
Gently replacing
In oblivion—

The Day Undressed Herself

The Day undressed—Herself—
Her Garter—was of Gold—
Her Petticoat—of Purple plain—
Her Dimities—as old

Exactly —as the World—
And yet the newest Star—
Enrolled upon the Hemisphere
Be wrinkled—much as Her—

Too near to God—to pray—
Too near to Heaven—to fear—
The Lady of the Occident
Retired without a care—

Her Candle so expire
The flickering be seen
On Ball of Mast in Bosporus—
And Dome—and Window Pane—

This World is Not Conclusion

This World is not Conclusion.
A Species stands beyond—
Invisible, as Music—
But positive, as Sound—
It beckons, and it baffles—
Philosophy—don't know—
And through a Riddle, at the last—
Sagacity, must go—
To guess it, puzzles scholars—
To gain it, Men have borne
Contempt of Generations
And Crucifixion, shown—

Faith slips—and laughs, and rallies—
Blushes, if any see —
Plucks at a twig of Evidence—
And asks a Vane, the way—
Much Gesture, from the Pulpit—
Strong Hallelujahs roll—
Narcotics cannot still the Tooth
That nibbles at the soul—

I Never Felt At Home Below

I never felt at Home—Below—
And in the Handsome Skies
I shall not feel at Home—I know—
I don't like Paradise—

Because it's Sunday—all the time—
And Recess—never comes—
And Eden'll be so lonesome
Bright Wednesday Afternoons—

If God could make a visit—
Or ever took a Nap—
So not to see us—but they say
Himself—a Telescope

Perennial beholds us—
Myself would run away
From Him—and Holy Ghost—and All—
But there's the "Judgement Day"!

A Visitor in Marl

A Visitor in Marl—
Who influences Flowers—
Till they are orderly as Busts—
And Elegant—as Glass—

Who visits in the Night—
And just before the Sun—
Concludes his glistening interview—
Caresses—and is gone—

But whom his fingers touched—
And where his feet have run—
And whatsoever Mouth he kissed—
Is as it had not been—

Alone I Cannot Be

Alone, I cannot be—
For Hosts—do visit me—
Recordless Company—
Who baffle Key—

They have no Robes, nor Names—
No Almanacs—nor Climes—
But general Homes
Like Gnomes—

Their Coming, may be known
By Couriers within—
Their going—is not—
For they're never gone—

The Robin's My Criterion For Tune

The Robin's my Criterion for Tune—
Because I grow—where Robins do—
But, were I Cuckoo born—
I'd swear by him—
The ode familiar—rules the Noon—
The Buttercup's, my Whim for Bloom—
Because, we're Orchard sprung—
But, were I Britian born,
I'd Daisies spurn—

None but the Nut-October fit—
Because, through dropping it,
The Seasons flit—I'm taught—
Without the Snow's Tableau
Winter, were lie—to me—
Because I see—New Englandly—
The Queen, discerns like me—
Provincially—

Behind Me Dips Eternity

Behind Me—dips Eternity—
Before Me—Immortality—
Myself—the Term between—
Death but the Drift of Eastern Gray,
Dissolving into Dawn away,
Before the West begin—

'Tis Kingdoms—afterward—they say—
In perfect—pauseless Monarchy—
Whose Prince—is Son of None—
Himself—His Dateless Dynasty—
Himself—Himself diversify—
In duplicate divine—

'Tis Miracle before Me—then—
'Tis Miracle behind—between—
A Crescent in the Sea—
With Midnight to the North of Her—
And Midnight to the South of Her—
And Maelstrom—in the Sky—

Because I Could Not Stop For Death

Because I could not stop for Death—
He kindly stopped for me—
The Carriage held but just Ourselves—
And Immortality.

We slowly drove—He knew no haste
And I had put away
My labor and my leisure too,
For His Civility—

We passed the School, where Children strove
At Recess—in the Ring—
We passed the Fields of Gazing Grain—
We passed the Setting Sun—

Or rather—He passed Us—
The Dews drew quivering and chill—
For only Gossamer, my Gown—
My Tippet—only Tulle—

We paused before a House that seemed
A Swelling of the Ground—

I Like To See It Lap the Miles

I like to see it lap the Miles—
And lick the Valleys up—
And stop to feed itself at Tanks—
And then—prodigious step

Around a Pile of Mountains—
And supercilious peer
In Shanties—by the sides of Roads—
And then a Quarry pare

To fit its Ribs—
And crawl between
Complaining all the while
In horrid—hooting stanza—
Then chase itself down Hill—

And neigh like Boanerges—
Then—punctual as—a Star
Stop—docile and omnipotent
At its own stable door—

I Never Saw a Moor

I never saw a Moor—
I never saw the Sea—
Yet know I how the Heather looks
And what a Billow be.

I never spoke with God
Nor visited in Heaven—
Yet certain am I of the spot
As if the Checks were given—

The Bustle in a House

The Bustle in a House
The Morning after Death
Is solemnest of industries
Enacted upon Earth—

The Sweeping up the Heart
And putting Love away
We shall not want to use again
Until Eternity.

A Route of Evanescence

A Route of Evanescence
With a revolving Wheel—
A Resonance of Emerald—
A Rush of Cochineal—
And every Blossom on the Bush
Adjusts it's tumbled Head—
The mail from Tunis, probably,
An easy Morning's Ride—

This is My Letter To The World

This is my letter to the World
That never wrote to Me—
The simple News that Nature told—
With tender Majesty

Her Message is committed
To Hands I cannot see—
For love of Her—Sweet—countrymen—
Judge tenderly—of Me

The Soul Selects Her Own Society

The Soul selects her own Society—
Then—shuts the Door—
To her divine Majority—
Present no more—

Unmoved—she notes the Chariots—pausing—
At her low Gate—
Unmoved—an Emperor be kneeling
Upon her Mat—

I've known her—from an ample nation—
Choose One—
Then—close the Valves of her attention—
Like Stone—

I Taste a Liquor Never Brewed

I taste a liquor never brewed—
From Tankards scooped in Pearl—
Not all the Vats upon the Rhine
Yield such an Alcohol!

Inebriate of Air—am I—
And Debauchee of Dew—
Reeling—thro endless summer days—
From inns of Molten Blue—

When "Landlords" turn the drunken Bee
Out of the Foxglove's door—
When Butterflies—renounce their "drams"—
I shall but drink the more!

Till Seraphs swing their snowy Hats—
And Saints—to windows run—
To see the little Tippler
Leaning against the—Sun—

My Life Closed Twice Before Its Close

My life closed twice before its close;
It yet remains to see
If Immortality unveil
A third event to me,

So huge, so hopeless to conceive
As these that twice befel.
Parting is all we know of heaven,
And all we need of hell.

Mine By The Right of the White Election

Mine—by the Right of the White Election!
Mine—by the Royal Seal!
Mine—by the Sign in the Scarlet prison—
Bars—cannot conceal!

Mine—here—in Vision—and in Veto!
Mine—by the Grave's Repeal—
Titled—Confirmed—
Delirious Charter!
Mine—long as Ages steal!

Bring Me the Sunset in a Cup

Bring me the sunset in a cup,
Reckon the morning's flagon's up
And say how many Dew,
Tell me how far the morning leaps—

Tell me what time the weaver sleeps
Who spun the breadths of blue!

Write me how many notes there be
In the new Robin's extasy
Among astonished boughs—
How many trips the Tortoise makes—
How many cups the Bee partakes,
The Debauchee of Dews!

Also, who laid the Rainbow's piers,
Also, who leads the docile spheres
By withes of supple blue?
Whose fingers string the stalactite—

Who counts the wampum of the night
To see that none is due?

Who built this little Alban House
And shut the windows down so close
My spirit cannot see?
Who'll let me out some gala day
With implements to fly away,
Passing Pomposity?

A Narrow Fellow in the Grass

A narrow fellow in the grass
Occasionally rides;
You may have met him,—did you not?
His notice sudden is.

The grass divides as with a comb,
A spotted shaft is seen;
And then it closes at your feet
And opens further on.

He likes a boggy acre,
A floor too cool for corn.
Yet when a child, and barefoot,
I more than once, at morn,

Have passed, I thought, a whip-lash
Unbraiding in the sun,—
When, stooping to secure it,
It wrinkled, and was gone.

Several of nature's people
I know, and they know me;
I feel for them a transport
Of cordiality;

But never met this fellow,
Attended or alone,
Without a tighter breathing,
And zero at the bone.

I Felt a Funeral in My Brain

I felt a funeral in my brain,
    And mourners, to and fro,
Kept treading, treading, till it seemed
    That sense was breaking through.

And when they all were seated,
    A service like a drum
Kept beating, beating, till I thought
    My mind was going numb.

And then I heard them lift a box,
    And creak across my soul
With those same boots of lead, again.
    Then space began to toll

As all the heavens were a bell,
    And Being but an ear,
And I and silence some strange race,
    Wrecked, solitary, here.

In Winter, in My Room

In winter, in my room,
I came upon a worm,
Pink, lank, and warm.
But as he was a worm
And worms presume,
Not quite with him at home—
Secured him by a string
To something neighboring,
And went along.

A trifle afterward
A thing occurred,
I'd not believe it if I heard—
But state with creeping blood;
A snake, with mottles rare,
Surveyed my chamber floor,
In feature as the worm before,
But ringed with power.
The very string
With which I tied him, too,
When he was mean and new,
That string was there.

I shrank—'How fair you are!'
Propitiation's claw—
'Afraid,' he hissed,
'Of me?'
'No cordiality?'
He fathomed me.
Then, to a rhythm slim
Secreted in his form,
As patterns swim,
Projected him.

That time I flew,
Both eyes his way,

Lest he pursue—
Nor ever ceased to run,
Till, in a distant town,
Towns on from mine—
I sat me down;
This was a dream.

I Meant to Have But Modest Needs

I meant to have but modest needs,
Such as content, and heaven;
Within my income these could lie,
And life and I keep even.

But since the last included both,
It would suffice my prayer
But just for one to stipulate,
And grace would grant the pair.

And so, upon this wise I prayed,—
Great Spirit, give to me
A heaven not so large as yours,
But large enough for me.

A smile suffused Jehovah's face;
The cherubim withdrew;
Grave saints stole out to look at me,
And showed their dimples, too.

I left the place with all my might,—
My prayer away I threw;
The quiet ages picked it up,
And Judgement twinkled, too.

That one so honest be extant
As take the tale for true

That "Whatsoever you shall ask,
Itself be given you."

But I, grown shrewder, scan the skies
With a suspicious air,—
As children, swindled for the first,
All swindlers be, infer.

I Cannot Live with You

I cannot live with you,
It would be life,
And life is over there
Behind the shelf

The sexton keeps the key to,
Putting up
Our life, his porcelain,
Like a cup

Discarded of the housewife,
Quaint or broken;
A newer Sévres pleases,
Old ones crack.

I could not die with you,
For one must wait
To shut the other's gaze down,—
You could not.

And I, could I stand by
And see you freeze,
Without my right of frost,
Death's privilege?

Nor could I rise with you,
Because your face

Would put out Jesus',
That new grace

Glow plain and foreign
On my homesick eye,
Except that you, than he
Shone closer by.

They'd judge us—how?
For you served Heaven, you know,
Or sought to;
I could not,

Because you saturated sight,
And I had no more eyes
For sordid excellence
As Paradise.

And were you lost, I would be,
Though my name
Rang loudest
On the heavenly fame.

And were you saved,
And I condemned to be
Where you were not,
That self were hell to me.

So we must keep apart,
You there, I here,
With just the door ajar
That oceans are,
And prayers,
And that pale sustenance,
Despair!

PAUL HAMILTON HAYNE [1830-1886]

Paul Hamilton Hayne was born in Charleston, South Carolina, to a family which provided him with numerous material, educational, and social advantages. He developed an early friendship with his schoolmate Henry Timrod and graduated from Charleston College at the age of twenty. He exhibited a special talent for literature and, as a result, became editor of the *Southern Literary Gazette*. In 1855, his *Poems* caught the interest of northern critics who had hitherto glanced only scathingly at writers from the South. Although he was sickly and his service in the military was brief, Hayne, like many of his contemporaries, was not spared considerable suffering during the war years, and after his ancestral home was destroyed by the armies of General Sherman, he decided to withdraw to the woods of Georgia. There he built a shack and undertook a new livelihood with his wife, Mary Middleton Michel, and his only child, William. Nevertheless, poetry remained an active interest, and much of his verse continued to find its way into numerous publications.

Aspects Of The Pines

Tall, sombre, grim, against the morning
        sky
  They rise, scarce touched by melancholy
        airs,
Which stir the fadeless foliage dream-
        fully,
  As if from realms of mystical despairs.

Tall, sombre, grim, they stand with dusky
        gleams

  Brightening to gold within the wood-
        land's core,
Beneath the gracious noontide's tranquil
        beams,—
  But the weird winds of morning sigh no
        more.

A stillness, strange, divine, ineffable,
  Broods round and o'er them in the wind's
        surcease,
And on each tinted copse and shimmering
        dell
  Rests the mute rapture of deep hearted
        peace.

Last, sunset comes—the solemn joy and
        might
  Borne from the west when cloudless day
        declines—
Low, flute-like breezes sweep the waves of
        light,
  And, lifting dark green tresses of the
        pines,

Till every lock is luminous, gently float,
  Fraught with hale odors up the heavens

afar,
To faint when twilight on her virginal
throat
Wears for a gem the tremulous vesper
star.

Vicksburg

For sixty days and upwards,
   A storm of shell and shot
Rained round us in a flaming shower,
   But still we faltered not.
"If the noble city perish,"
   Our grand young leader said,
"Let the only walls the foe shall scale
   Be ramparts of the dead !"

For sixty days and upwards,
   The eye of heaven waxed dim;
And even throughout God's holy morn,
   O'er Christian prayer and hymn,
Arose a hissing tumult,
   As if the fiends in air
Strove to engulf the voice of faith
   In the shrieks of their despair.

There was wailing in the houses,
   There was trembling on the marts,
While the tempest raged and thundered,
   Mid the silent thrill of hearts;
But the Lord, our shield, was with us,
   And ere a month had sped,
our very women walked the streets
   With scarce one throb of dread.

And the little children gambolled,
    Their faces purely raised,
Just for a wondering moment,
    As the huge bombs whirled and blazed;
Then turned with silvery laughter
    To the sports which children love,
Thrice-mailed in the sweet, instinctive
        thought
    That the good God watched above.

Yet the hailing bolts fell faster,
    From scores of flame-clad ships,
And about us, denser, darker,
    Grew the conflict's wild eclipse,
Till a solid cloud closed o'er us,
    Like a type of doom and ire,
Whence shot a thousand quivering tongues
    Of forked and vengeful fire.

But the unseen hands of angels
    Those death-shafts warned aside,
And the dove of heavenly mercy
    Ruled o'er the battle tide;
In the houses ceased the wailing,
    And through the war-scarred marts
The people strode, with step of hope,
    To the music in their hearts.

Between The Sunken Sun
and The New Moon

Between the sunken sun and the new
          moon,
I stood in fields through which a rivulet
          ran
With scarce perceptible motion, not a span
Of its smooth surface trembling to the tune
Of sunset breezes: "O delicious boon,"
I cried, "of quiet ! wise is Nature's plan,
Who, in her realm, as in the soul of man,
Alternates storm with calm, and the loud
          noon
With dewy evening's soft and sacred lull:
Happy the heart that keeps *its* twilight
          hour,
And, in the depths of heavenly peace re-
          clined,
Loves to commune with thoughts of tender
          power;
Thoughts that ascend, like angels beauti-
          ful,
A shining Jacob's ladder of the mind."

The Mocking-Birds

Oh, all day long they flood with song
    The forest shades, the fields of light;
Heaven's heart is stilled and strangely thrilled
    By ecstasies of lyric might;
From flower-crowned nooks of spendid dyes,
    Lone dells a shadowy quiet girds;
Far echoes, wakening, gently rise,
And o'er the woodland track send back
    Soft answers to the mocking-birds.

The winds, in awe, no gusty flaw
    Dare breathe in rhythmic Beauty's face;
Nearer the pale-gold cloudlets draw
    Above a charmed, melodious place:
Entrancéd Nature listening knows
    No music set to mortal words,
Nor nightingales that woo the rose,
Can vie with these deep harmonies
    Poured from the minstrel mocking-birds.

But, vaguely seen through gulfs of green,
    We glimpse the plumed and choral throng—
Sole poets born whose instincts scorn
    To do Song's lowliest utterance wrong:
Whate'er they sing, a sylvan art,
    On each wild, wood-born note conferred,
Guides the hot brain and hurtling heart.
Oh magical flame, whence pulsing came
    This passion of the mocking-bird?

Aye—pause and hark—be still, and mark
    What countless grades of voice and tone
From bosk and tree, from strand and sea,
    These small, winged genii make their own:
Fine lyric memories live again,

From tuneful burial disinterred,
To magnify the fiery strain
Which quivering trills and smites the hills
    With rapture of the mocking-bird.

Aye—pause and hark—be still, and mark
    How downward borne from Song's high clime
(No loftier haunts the English lark)
    They revel, each a jocund mime:
Their glad sides shake in bush and brake;
    And farm-girls, bowed o'er cream and curd,
Glance up to smile, and think the while
Of all blithe things that flit on wings
    None match the jovial mocking-bird.

When fun protrudes gay interludes
    Of blissful, glorious unrestraint,
They run, all wild with motley moods,
    Thro' Mirth's rare gamut, sly and quaint:
Humors grotesque and arabesque
    Flash up from spirits brightly stirred;
And even the pedant at his desk,
Feeling in turn his spirit burn,
    Laughs with the loudest mocking-bird.

Oh, all day long the world with song
    Is flooded, till the twilight dim;
What time its whole mysterious soul
    Seems rippling to the conscious brim:
Arcadian Eve through tranquil skies
    Pastures her stars in radiant herds;
And still the unwearied echoes rise,
And down a silvery track send back
    Fond greeting to the mocking-bird.

At last, fair boon, the summer moon
    Beyond the hazed horizon shines;
Ah, soon through night they wing their flight

To coverts of Aeolian pines:
A tremulous hush—then sweet and grand,
    From depths the dense, fair foliage girds,
Their love notes fill the enchanted land;
Through leaf-wrought bars they storm the stars,
These love songs of the mocking-birds.

A Little While I Fain Would Linger Yet

A little while (my life is almost set!)
    I fain would pause along the downward way,
    Musing an hour in this sad sunset-ray,
While, Sweet! our eyes with tender tears are wet:
A little hour I fain would linger yet.

A little while I fain would linger yet,
    All for love's sake, for love that cannot tire;
    Though fervid youth be dead, with youth's desire,
And hope has faded to a vague regret,
A little while I fain would linger yet.

A little while I fain would linger here:
    Behold! who knows what strange, mysterious bars
    'Twixt souls that love may rise in other stars?
Nor can love deem the face of death is fair:
A little while I still would linger here.

A little while I yearn to hold thee fast,
    Hand locked in hand, and loyal heart to heart;
    (O pitying Christ! those woeful words, *"We part!"*)
So ere the darkness fall, the light be past,
A little while I fain would hold thee fast.

A little while, when night and twilight meet:

Behind, our broken years; before, the deep
Weird wonder of the last unfathomed sleep.
A little while I still would clasp thee, Sweet;
A little while, when night and twilight meet.

A little while I fain would linger here;
Behold! who knows what soul-dividing bars
Earth's faithful loves may part in other stars?
Nor can love deem the face of death is fair:
A little while I still would linger here.

MARY MAPES DODGE [1831-1905]

Mary Mapes Dodge was born and raised in New York City. As the daughter of a prominent scientist, she was educated at home by private tutors and grew up in a stimulating environment among many of the most successful people of the time. She married at age twenty and had two sons. After her husband's untimely death, she was able to make a living as a writer and poet. In particular, she gained widespread popularity as a children's author. Although she is best known for her story *Hans Brinker,* her poetry has qualities which should not be overlooked; it is written in a style which is refreshing, quaint, and reflects a delicate balance of humor and sophistication.

Once Before

Once before, this self-same air
Passed me, though I know not where.
Strange ! how very like it came !
Touch and fragrance were the same;
Sound of mingled voices, too,
With a light laugh ringing through;
Some one moving, here and there,—
Some one passing up the stair,
Some one calling from without,
Or a far-off childish shout,—
Simple, home-like, nothing more,
Yet it all hath been before !

No: not to-day, nor yesterday,
Nor any day ! But far away—
So long ago, so very far.

It might have been on other star.
How was it spent ? and where ? and when ?
This life that went, yet comes again ?
Was sleep its world, or death its shore ?
I still the silent Past implore.
Ah ! never dream had power to show
Such vexing glimpse of Long Ago.
Never a death could follow death
With love between, and home, and breath.

The spell has passed. What spendthrifts we
Of simple, household certainty !
What golden grain we trample low
Searching for flowers that never grow !
Why, home is real, and love is real;
Nor false our honest high ideal.
Life,—it is bounding, warm, and strong,—
And all my heart resounds with song.
It must be true, whate'er befall,

This and the world to come are all.
And yet it puzzles me—alack !—
When life that could not be, comes back !

The Stars

They wait all day unseen by us, unfelt;
Patient they bide behind the day's full glare;
And we, who watched the dawn when they
            were there,
Thought we had seen them in the daylight
            melt,
While the slow sun upon the earth-line
            knelt.
Because the teeming sky seemed void and
            bare,
When we explored it through the dazzled
            air,
We had no thought that there all day they
            dwelt.
Yet were they over us, alive and true,
In the vast shades far up above the blue,—
The brooding shades beyond our daylight
            ken,—
Serene and patient in their conscious light,
Ready to sparkle for our joy again,—
The eternal jewels of the short-lived night.

Emerson

We took it to the woods, we two,
　　The book well worn and brown,
To read his words where stirring leaves
　　Rained their soft shadows down.

Yet as we sat and breathed the scene,
　　We opened not a page;
Enough that he was with us there,
　　Our silent, friendly sage !

His fresh "Rhodora" bloomed again;
　　His "Humble-bee" buzzed near;
And oh, the "Wood-notes" beautiful
　　He taught our souls to hear.

So our unopened book was read;
　　And so, in restful mood,
We and our poet, arm in arm,
Went sauntering through the wood.

Shadow-Evidence

Swift o'er the sunny grass,
    I saw a shadow pass
    With subtle charm,—
So quick, so full of life
With thrilling joy so rife,
I started lest, unknown,
My step—ere it was flown—
    Had done it harm.

Why look up to the blue ?
The bird was gone, I knew,
    Far out of sight.
Steady and keen of wing,
The slight, impassioned thing,
Intent on a goal unknown,
Had held its course alone
    In silent flight.

Dear little bird, and fleet,
Flinging down at my feet
    Shadow for song:
More sure am I of thee—
Unseen, unheard by me—
Than of some things felt and known,
And guarded as my own,
All my life long.

Snow-Flakes

Whenever a snow-flake leaves the sky,
It turns and turns to say "Good-bye!
Good-bye, dear clouds, so cool and gray!"
Then lightly travels on its way.

And when a snow-flake finds a tree,
"Good-day!" it says—"Good-day to thee!
Thou art so bare, and lonely, dear,
I'll rest and call my comrades here."

But when a snow-flake, brave and meek,
Lights on a rosy maiden's cheek,
It starts—"How warm and soft the day!
'T is summer!"—and it melts away.

ELIZABETH AKERS ALLEN [1832-1911]

Elizabeth Akers Allen was born in upstate New York. In spite of a somewhat turbulent personal life, she was able to establish herself as a successful figure in the literary world. After her first marriage ended in divorce, she became a newspaper editor and wrote poetry which was published under the pseudonym "Florence Percy"; later on, she adopted the penname "Mrs. Akers". While traveling in Europe, she met and married a sculptor. Life among foreign artists and intellectuals, however, did not last; her husband died, and she returned home only to settle down again as an editor and to marry E.M. Allen, her third spouse. The poetry she produced tends to be sentimental and, as a result, is less appealing today than it might have been at the time of publication. Elizabeth Akers Allen is perhaps best known for her poem "Rock Me To Sleep" published in 1859.

Sea-Birds

O lonesome sea -gull, floating far
  Over the ocean's icy waste,
Aimless and wide thy wanderings are,
  Forever vainly seeking rest;—
  Where is thy mate, and where thy
    nest?

'Twixt wintry sea and wintry sky,
  Cleaving the keen air with thy breast,
Thou sailest slowly, solemnly;
  No fetter on thy wing is pressed:—
  Where is thy mate, and where thy
    nest?

O restless, homeless human soul,
  Following for aye thy nameless quest,
The gulls float, and the billows roll;
  Thou watchest still, and questionest:—
  Where is *thy* mate, and where thy
    nest?

My Dearling

My Dearling !—thus, in days long fled,
  In spite of creed and court and queen,
  King Henry wrote to Anne Boleyn,—
The dearest pet name ever said,
  And dearly purchased, too, I ween !

Poor child ! she played a losing game:
  She won a heart,—so Henry said,—
  But ah, the price she gave instead !
Men's hearts, at best, are but a name:
  She paid for Henry's with her head !

You count men's hearts as something
        worth ?
Not I: were I a maid unwed,
I'd rather have my own fair head
Than all the lovers on the earth,
    Than all the hearts that ever bled !

"My Dearling !" with a love most true,
    Having no fear of creed or queen,
    I breathe that name my prayers between;
But it shall never bring to you
    The hapless fate of Anne Boleyn !

Rock Me to Sleep [1860]

Backward, turn backward, O Time, in your flight,
Make me a child again just for to-night!
Mother, come back from the echoless shore,
Take me again to your heart as of yore;
Kiss from my forehead the furrows of care,
Smooth the few silver threads out of my hair;
Over my slumbers your loving watch keep;—
Rock me to sleep, mother,—rock me to sleep!

Backward, flow backward, O tide of the years!
I am so weary of toil and of tears,—
Toil without recompense, tears all in vain,—
Take them, and give me my childhood again!
I have grown weary of dust and decay,—
Weary of flinging my soul-wealth away;
Weary of sowing for others to reap;—
Rock me to sleep, mother,—rock me to sleep!

Tired of the hollow, the base, the untrue,
Mother, O mother, my heart calls for you!
Many a summer the grass has grown green,

Blossomed and faded, our faces between:
Yet, with strong yearning and passionate pain,
Long I to-night for your presence again.
Come from the silence so long and so deep;—
Rock me to sleep, mother,—rock me to sleep!

Over my heart, in the days that are flown,
No love like mother-love ever has shown;
No other worship abides and endures,—
Faithful, unselfish, and patient like yours:
None like a mother can charm away pain
From the sick soul and the world-weary brain.
Slumber's soft calms o'er my heavy lids creep;—
Rock me to sleep, mother,—rock me to sleep!

Come, let your brown hair, just lighted with gold,
Fall on your shoulders again as of old;
Let it drop over my forehead to-night,
Shading my faint eyes away from the light;
For with its sunny-edged shadows once more
Haply will throng the sweet visions of yore;
Lovingly, softly, its bright billows sweep;—
Rock me to sleep, mother,—rock me to sleep!

Mother, dear mother, the years have been long
Since I last listened your lullaby song:
Sing, then, and unto my soul it shall seem
Womanhood's years have been only a dream.
Clasped to your heart in a loving embrace,
With your light lashes just sweeping my face,
Never hereafter to wake or to weep;—
Rock me to sleep, mother,—rock me to sleep!

The Telltale

Once, on a golden afternoon,
With radiant faces and hearts in tune,
    Two fond lovers in dreaming mood
    Threaded a rural solitude.
Wholly happy, they only knew
That the earth was bright and the sky was blue,
    That light and beauty and joy and song
    Charmed the way as they passed along:
The air was fragrant with woodland scents;
The squirrel frisked on the roadside fence;
    And hovering near them, "Chee, chee,
      chink?"
    Queried the curious bobolink,
Pausing and peering with sidelong head,
As saucily questioning all they said;
    While the ox-eye danced on its slender stem,
    And all glad nature rejoiced with them.
Over the odorous fields were strown
Wilting windrows of grass new-mown,
    And rosy billows of clover bloom
    Surged in the sunshine and breathed perfume.
Swinging low on a slender limb,
The sparrow warbled his wedding hymn,
    And, balancing on a blackberry-brier,
    The bobolink sung with his heart on fire,—
"Chink? If you wish to kiss her, do!
Do it, do it! You coward, you!
    Kiss her! Kiss, kiss her! Who will see?
    Only we three! we three! we three!"
Under garlands of drooping vines,
Through dim vistas of sweet breathed pines,
    Past wide meadow-fields, lately mowed,
    Wandered the indolent country road.
The lovers followed it, listening still,
And, loitering slowly, as lovers will,
    Entered a low-roofed bridge that lay,
    Dusky and cool, in their pleasant way.

Under its arch a smooth, brown stream
Silently glided, with glint and gleam,
    Shaded by graceful elms that spread
    Their verdurous canopy overhead,—
The stream so narrow, the boughs so wide,
They met and mingled across the tide.
    Alders loved it, and seemed to keep
    Patient watch as it lay asleep,
Mirroring clearly the trees and sky
And the flitting form of the dragon-fly,
    Save where the swift-winged swallow played
    In and out in the sun and shade,
And darting and circling in merry chase,
Dipped and dimpled its clear dark face.

Fluttering lightly from brink to brink
Followed the garrulous bobolink,
    Rallying loudly, with mirthful din,
    The pair who lingered unseen within.
And when from the friendly bridge at last
Into the road beyond they passed,
    Again beside them the tempter went,
    Keeping the thread of his argument:—
"Kiss her! kiss her! chink-a-chee-chee!
I'll not mention it! Don't mind me!
    I'll be sentinel—I can see
    All around from this tall birch tree!"

But ah! they noted—nor deemed it strange—
In his rollicking chorus a trifling change:
    "Do it! do it!" with might and main
    Warbled the telltale—"Do it *again*!"

ANNIE ADAMS FIELDS [1834-1915]

Annie Adams Fields was born in Boston to an educated, well-to-do family. At twenty, she married James T. Fields, a distinguished publisher who was seventeen years her senior. Almost immediately, the new couple's home became a favorite gathering place. During her early married years, Fields kept a journal in which she recorded many of her experiences among prominent personalities in society and business. This diary subsequently provided the material for the further development of her thoughts in poetry and fiction. Although Fields began as a writer of prose, she eventually moved to poetry. Her major publications include *Under the Olive, The Singing Shepherd and Other Poems,* and *Orpheus: A Masque.*

*On Waking From A
Dreamless Sleep*

I waked; the sun was in the sky,
    The face of heaven was fair;
The silence all about me lay,
    Of morning in the air.

I said, Where hast thou been, my soul,
Since the moon set in the west ?
I know not where thy feet have trod,
    Nor what has been thy quest.

Where wast thou when Orion past
    Below the dark-blue sea ?
His glittering, silent stars are gone,—
    Didst follow them for me ?

Where wast thou in that awful hour
    When first the night-wind heard
The faint breath of the coming dawn,
    And fled before the word ?

Where hast thou been, my spirit,
    Since the long wave on the shore
Tenderly rocked my sense asleep,
    And I heard thee no more ?

My limbs like breathing marble
    Have lain in the warm down;
No heavenly chant, no earthly care,
    Have stirred a smile or frown.

I wake; thy kiss is on my lips;
    Thou art my day, my sun !
But where, O spirit, where wast thou
    While the sands of night have run ?

Theocritus

Ay! Unto thee belong
The pipe and song,
Theocritus,—
Loved by the satyr and the faun !
To thee the olive and the vine,
To thee the Mediterranean pine,
And the soft lapping sea !
Thine, Bacchus,
Thine, the blood-red revels,
Thine, the bearded goat !
Soft valleys unto thee,
And Aphrodite's shrine,
And maidens veiled in falling robes of lawn !
But unto us, to us
The stalwart glories of the North;
Ours is the sounding main,
And ours the voices uttering forth
By midnight round these cliffs a mighty
                    strain;
A tale of viewless islands in the deep
Washed by the waves' white fire;
Of mariners rocked asleep,
In the great cradle, far from Grecian ire
Of Neptune and his train;
To us, to us,
The dark-leaved shadow and the shining
                    birch,
The flight of gold through hollow wood-
                    lands driven,
Soft dying of the year with many a sigh,
These, all, to us are given !
And eyes that eager evermore shall search
The hidden seed, and searching find again
Unfading blossoms of a fadeless spring;
These, these, to us !
The sacred youth and maid,
Coy and half afraid;

The sorrowful earthly pall,
Winter and wintry rain,
And autumn's gathered grain,
With whispering music in their fall;
These unto us !
And unto thee, Theocritus,
To thee,
The immortal childhood of the world,
The laughing waters of an inland sea,
And beckoning signal of a sail unfurled !

Little Guinever

"When Queen Guinever of Britain was a little wench."
LOVE'S LABOUR'S LOST.

Swift across the palace floor
    Flashed her tiny wilful feet;
"Playfellow, I will no more,
    Now I must my task complete."

Arthur kissed her childish hand,
    Sighed to think her task severe,
Walked forth in the garden land,
    Lonely till she reappear.

She has sought her latticed room,
    Overlooking faery seas,
Called Launcelot from a bowery gloom
    To feast of milk and honey of bees.

"Had we bid Prince Arthur too,
    He had shaken his grave head,
Saying, 'My holidays are few !'—
    May queens not have their will ?" she said.

Thus she passed the merry day,
   Thus her women spake and smiled:
"All we see we need not say,
   For Guinever is but a child."

The Return

The bright sea washed beneath her feet,
   As it had done of yore,
The well-remembered odor sweet
   Came through her opening door.

Again the grass his ripened head
   Bowed where her raiment swept;
Again the fog-bell told of dread,
   And all the landscape wept.

Again beside the woodland bars
   She found the wilding rose,
With petals fine and heart of stars,—
   The flower our childhood knows.

And there, before that blossom small,
   By its young face beguiled,
The woman saw her burden fall,
   And stood a little child.

She knew no more the weight of love,
   No more the weight of grief;
So could the simple wild-rose move
   And bring her heart relief.

She asked not where her love was gone,
   Nor where her grief was fled,
But stood as at the great white throne,
   Unmindful of things dead.

*Song, to the Gods, is
Sweetest Sacrifice*

"Behold another singer !" Criton said,
And sneered, and in his sneering turned
    the leaf:
"Who reads the poets now ? They are
    past and dead:
Give me for their vain work unrhymed re-
    lief."
A laugh went round. Meanwhile the last
    ripe sheaf
Of corn was garnered, and the summer
    birds
Stilled their dear notes, while autumn's
    voice of grief
Rang through the fields, and wept the
    gathered herds.
Then in despair men murmured: "Is this
    all,—
To fade and die within this narrow ring ?
Where are the singers, with their hearts
    aflame,
To tell again what those of old let
    fall,—
How to decaying worlds fresh promise
    came,
And how our angels in the night-time
    sing ?"

LOUISE CHANDLER MOULTON [1835-1908]

Louise Chandler Moulton was the only surviving child of an upper-class, rigidly Calvinistic family. She married the journalist and publisher, William Hugh Moulton, and spent all of her life in Boston. Moulton began to write poetry at the early age of seven, and her first poem was published when she was fifteen. In due time, she became a respected figure in the literary and cultural circles of Massachusetts. Although she was known primarily as a poet of sonnets, she was also an experienced editor and a prolific writer of children's literature.

To-Night

Bend low, O dusky Night,
    And give my spirit rest.
    Hold me to your deep breast,
And put old cares to flight.
Give back the lost delight
    That once my soul possest,
    When Love was loveliest.
Bend low, O dusky Night!

Enfold me in your arms—
    The sole embrace I crave
    Until the embracing grave
Shield me from life's alarms.
I dare your subtlest charms;
    Your deepest spell I brave,—
    O, strong to slay or save,
Enfold me in your arms!

A Painted Fan

Roses and butterflies snared on a fan,
    All that is left of a summer gone by;
Of swift, bright wings that flashed in the
        sun,
    And loveliest blossoms that bloomed to
        die!

By what subtle spell did you lure them
        here,
    Fixing a beauty that will not change,—
Roses whose petals never will fall,
    Bright, swift wings that never will range?

Had you owned but the skill to snare as
        well

The swift-winged hours that came and
            went,
To prison the words that in music died,
    And fix with a spell the heart's content,

Then had you been of magicians the chief
    And loved and lovers should bless your
            art,
If you could but have painted the soul of
            the thing,—
    Not the rose alone, but the rose's heart!

Flown are those days with their winged de-
            lights,
    As the odor is gone from the summer
            rose;
Yet still, whenever I wave my fan,
    The soft, south wind of memory blows.

The Shadow Dance

She sees her image in the glass,—
    How fair a thing to gaze upon!
    She lingers while the moments run,
With happy thoughts that come and pass,

Like winds across the meadow grass
    When the young June is just begun:
She sees her image in the glass,—
    How fair a thing to gaze upon!

What wealth of gold the skies amass!
    How glad are all things 'neath the
            sun !
    How true the love her love has won!
She recks not that this hour will pass,—
She sees her image in the glass.

Laus Veneris

A PICTURE BY BURNE JONES

Pallid with too much longing,
　　White with passion and prayer,
Goddess of love and beauty,
　　She sits in the picture there,—

Sits with her dark eyes seeking
　　Something more subtle still
Than the old delights of loving
　　Her measureless days to fill.

She has loved and been loved so often
　　In her long, immortal years,
That she tires of the worn-out rapture,
　　Sickens of hopes and fears.

No joys or sorrows move her,
　　Done with her ancient pride;
For her head she found too heavy
　　The crown she has cast aside.

Clothed in her scarlet splendor,
　　Bright with her glory of hair,
Sad that she is not mortal,—
　　Eternally sad and fair,

Longing for joys she knows not,
　　Athirst with a vain desire,
There she sits in the picture,
　　Daughter of foam and fire.

Hic Jacet

So love is dead that has been quick so long!
Close, then, his eyes, and bear him to his rest,
With eglantine and myrtle on his breast,

And leave him there, their pleasant scents among;
And chant a sweet and melancholy song
About the charms whereof he was possessed,
And how of all things he was loveliest,
And to compare with aught were him to wrong.
Leave him beneath the still and solemn stars,
That gather and look down from their far place
With their long calm our brief woes to deride,
Until the Sun the Morning's gate unbars
And mocks, in turn, our sorrows with his face;—
And yet, had Love been Love, he had not died.

At Midsummer

The spacious Noon enfolds me with its peace—
    The affluent Midsummer wraps me round—
    So still the earth and air, that scarce a sound
Affronts the silence, and the swift caprice
Of one stray bird's lone call does but increase
    The sense of some compelling hush profound,
    Some spell by which the whole vast world is bound,
Till star-crowned Night smile downward its release.

I sit and dream—midway of the long day—
    Midway of the glad year—midway of life—
        My whole world seems, indeed, to hold its
            breath:—

For me the sun stands still upon his way—
    The winds for one short hour remit their strife—
        Then Day, and Year, and Life whirl on toward
            Death.

THOMAS BAILEY ALDRICH [1836-1907]

Thomas Bailey Aldrich was born in Portsmouth, New Hampshire, but spent much of his early life in New York and New Orleans. His family had hoped to send him to Harvard; this, however, did not happen on account of his father's death in 1849 and the financial circumstances which followed. Instead, Aldrich turned to composing verse for magazines and cultivating literary friendships. In 1855, after the publication of a first book of poems, he became a critic for the *Evening Mirror* and began a successful career as a journalist and writer. By 1865, he had married and decided to settle in Boston, a city associated with the activity of prominent literary figures such as Longfellow, Holmes, and Emerson. During his productive, prosperous years in the new home, he developed a poetic style which was acclaimed for its unusual grace and superb worksmanship. Among his well-known works are "The Bells" (1885), "Pampinea" (1861), "Cloth of Gold" (1874), "Flower and Thorn" (1877), "Friar Jerome's Beautiful Book" (1881), and "Windham Towers" (1890).

Appreciation

To the sea-shell's spiral round
'T is your heart that brings the sound:
The soft sea-murmurs that you hear
Within, are captured from your ear.

You do poets and their song
A grievous wrong,
If your own soul does not bring
To their high imagining
As much beauty as they sing.

To Hafiz

Though gifts like thine the fates gave not
            to me,
One thing, O Hafiz, we both hold in fee —
Nay, it holds us; for when the June wind
            blows
We both are slaves and lovers to the rose.
In vain the pale Circassian lily shows
Her face at her green lattice, and in vain
The violet beckons, with unveilèd face—
The bosom's white, the lips light purple
            stain,
These touch our liking, yet no passion stir.
But when the rose comes, Hafiz—in that
            place
Where she stands smiling, we kneel down
            to her !

When the Sultan Goes to Ispahan

When the Sultan Shah-Zaman
Goes to the city Ispahan,
Even before he gets so far
As the place where the clustered palm-
            trees are,
At the last of the thirty palace-gates,
The flower of the harem, Rose-in-Bloom,
Orders a feast in his favorite room—
Glittering squares of colored ice,
Sweetened with syrop, tinctured with spice,
Creams, and cordials, and sugared dates,
Syrian apples, Othmanee quinces,
Limes, and citrons, and apricots,
And wines that are known to Eastern
            princes;
And Nubian slaves, with smoking pots
Of spicëd meats and costliest fish
And all that the curious palate could wish,
Pass in and out of the cedarn doors;
Scattered over mosaic floors
Are anemones, myrtles, and violets,
And a musical fountain throws its jets
Of a hundred colors into the air.
The dusk Sultana loosens her hair,
And stains with the henna-plant the tips
Of her pointed nails, and bites her lips
Till they bloom again; but, alas, *that* rose
Not for the Sultan buds and blows,
Not for the Sultan Shah-Zaman
When he goes to the city Ispahan.

Then at a wave of her sunny hand
The dancing-girls of Samarcand
Glide in like shapes from fairy-land,
Making a sudden mist in air
Of fleecy veils and floating hair
And white arms lifted. Orient blood

Runs in their veins, shines in their eyes.
And there, in this Eastern Paradise,
Filled with the breath of sandal-wood,
And Khoten musk, and aloes and myrrh,
Sits Rose-in-Bloom on a silk divan,
Sipping the wines of Astrakhan;
And her Arab lover sits with her.
That's when the Sultan Shah-Zaman
Goes to the city Ispahan.

Now, when I see an extra light,
Flaming, flickering on the night
From my neighbor's casement opposite,
I know as well as I know to pray,
I know as well as a tongue can say,
That the innocent Sultan Shah-Zaman
Has gone to the city Ispahan.

Reminiscence

Though I am native to this frozen zone
That half the twelvemonth torpid lies, or dead;
Though the cold azure arching overhead
And the Atlantic's never-ending moan
Are mine by heritage, I must have known
Life otherwise in epochs long since fled;
For in my veins some Orient blood is red,
And through my thought are lotus blossoms blown.
I do remember. . . it was just at dusk,
Near a walled garden at the river's turn
(A thousand summers seem but yesterday!),
A Nubian girl, more sweet than Khoorja musk,
Came to the water-tank to fill her urn,
And, with the urn, she bore my heart away.

Heredity

A soldier of the Cromwell stamp,
With sword and psalm-book by his side,
At home alike in church and camp:
Austere he lived, and smileless died.

But she, a creature soft and fine—
From Spain, some say, some say from France;
Within her veins leapt blood like wine—
She led her Roundhead lord a dance!

In Grantham church they lie asleep;
Just where, the verger may not know.
Strange that two hundred years should keep
The old ancestral fires aglow!

In me these two have met again;
To each my nature owes a part:
To one, the cool and reasoning brain;
To one, the quick, unreasoning heart.

Pampinea [1861]

AN IDYL

Lying by the summer sea
I had a dream of Italy.
        Chalky cliffs and miles of sand,
Mossy reefs and salty caves,
Then the sparkling emerald waves,
Faded: and I seemed to stand,
Myself a languid Florentine,
In the heart of that fair land.
And in a garden cool and green,
Boccaccio's own enchanted place,
I met Pampinea, face to face—

A maid so lovely that to see
Her smile is to know Italy!
Her hair was like a coronet
Upon her Grecian forehead set,
Where one gem glistened sunnily
Like Venice, when first seen at sea!
I saw within her violet eyes
The starlight of Italian skies,
And on her brow and breast and hand
The olive of her native land.
And knowing how in other times
Her lips were ripe with Tuscan rhymes
Of love and wine and dance, I spread
My mantle by an almond tree,
"And here, beneath the rose," I said,
"I'll hear thy Tuscan melody!"
I heard a tale that was not told
In those ten dreamy days of old,
When Heaven for some divine offence,
Smote Florence with the pestilence;
And in that garden's odorous shade,
The dames of the Decameron,
With each a loyal lover, strayed,
To laugh and sing, at sorest need,
To lie in the lilies in the sun
With glint of plume and silver brede!
And while she whispered in my ear,
The pleasant Arno murmured near,
The dewy, slim chameleons run
Through twenty colors in the sun;
The breezes broke the fountain's glass,
And woke aeolian melodies,
And shook from out the scented trees
The lemon-blossoms on the grass.
The tale? I have forgot the tale!
A Lady all for love forlorn,
A rose-bud, and a nightingale
That bruised his bosom on the thorn;
A pot of rubies buried deep,

A glen, a corpse, a child asleep,
A Monk, that was no monk at all,
In the moonlight by a castle wall.
     Now while the large-eyed Tuscan wove
The glided thread of her romance—
Which I have lost by grievous chance—
The one dear woman that I love,
Beside me in our seaside nook,
Closed a white finger in her book,
Half vext that she should read, and weep
For Petrarch, to a man asleep!
And scorning me, so tame and cold,
She rose, and wandered down the shore,
Her wine-dark drapery, fold in fold,
Imprisoned by an ivory hand;
And on a ledge of oölite, half in sand,
She stood, and looked at Appledore.
     And waking, I beheld her there
Sea-dreaming in the moted air,
A siren lithe and debonair,
With wristlets woven of scarlet weeds,
And oblong lucent amber beads
Of sea-kelp shining in her hair.
And as I thought of dreams, and how
The something in us never sleeps,
But laughs, or sings, or moans, or weeps,
She turned—and on her breast and brow
I saw the tint that seemed not won
From kisses of New England sun;
I saw on brow and breast and hand
The olive of a sunnier land!
She turned—and, lo! within her eyes
There lay the starlight of Italian skies!
     Most dreams are dark, beyond the range
Of reason; oft we cannot tell
If they are born of heaven or hell:
But to my soul it seems not strange
That, lying by the summer sea,

With that dark woman watching me,
I slept and dreamed of Italy!

Broken Music

"A note all out of tune in this world's instrument." —AMY LEVY

I know not in what fashion she was made,
    Nor what her voice was, when she used to speak,
Nor if the silken lashes threw a shade
        On wan or rosy cheek.

I picture her with sorrowful vague eyes
    Illumed with such strange gleams of inner light
As linger in the drift of London skies
        Ere twilight turns to night.

I know not; I conjecture. 'T was a girl
    That with her own most gentle desperate hand
From out God's mystic setting plucked life's pearl—
        'Tis hard to understand.

So precious life is! Even to the old
    The hours are as a miser's coins, and she—
Within her hands lay youth's unminted gold
        And all felicity.

The winged impetuous spirit, the white flame
That was her soul once, whither has it flown?

Above her brow gray lichens blot her name
        Upon the carven stone.

This is her Book of Verses—wren-like notes,
   Shy franknesses, blind gropings, haunting fears;
At times across the chords abruptly floats
      A mist of passionate tears.

A fragile lyre too tensely keyed and strung,
   A broken music, weirdly incomplete;
Here a proud mind, self-baffled and self-stung,
      Lies coiled in dark defeat.

Outward Bound

I leave behind me the elm-shadowed square
And carven portals of the silent street,
And wander on with listless, vagrant feet
Through seaward-leading alleys, till the air
Smells of the sea, and straightway then the care
Slips from my heart, and life once more is sweet.
At the lane's ending lie the white-winged fleet.
O restless Fancy, whither wouldst thou fare?
Here are brave pinions that shall take thee far—
Gaunt hulks of Norway; ships of red Ceylon;
Slim-masted lovers of the blue Azores!
'T is but an instant hence to Zanzibar,
Or to the regions of the Midnight Sun.
Ionian isles are thine, and all the fairy shores!

EDWARD ROWLAND SILL [1841-1887]

Born in Windsor, Connecticut, Edward Rowland Sills lost his parents at an early age. Although he was a frail and hypersensitive young man, he was able to attend Yale University; there he began to develop an interest in writing poetry and produced some works which have since been hailed as being among his best. As a student, he was involved in the production of local literary magazines. But after graduation, he tried various careers before settling as a professor of English at the University of California. Although he continued to publish, especially under the pseudonym "Andrew Hedbrooke", declining health eventually began to curtail his output. During his lifetime, he produced only one volume of poetry in which "The Fool's Prayer" and "Opportunity" are among the better selections. His works are masterful but are often considered cold and passionless.

The Fool's Prayer

The royal feast was done; the King
 Sought some new sport to banish care,
And to his jester cried: "Sir Fool,
 Kneel now, and make for us a prayer!"

The jester doffed his cap and bells,
 And stood the mocking court before;
They could not see the bitter smile
 Behind the painted grin he wore.

He bowed his head, and bent his knee
 Upon the monarch's silken stool;
His pleading voice arose: "O Lord,
 Be merciful to me, a fool!

"No pity, Lord, could change the heart
 From red with wrong to white as wool:
The rod must heal the sin; but, Lord,
 Be merciful to me, a fool!

"'Tis not by guilt the onward sweep
 Of truth and right, O Lord, we stay;
'Tis by our follies that so long
 We hold the earth from heaven away.

"These clumsy feet, still in the mire,
 Go crushing blossoms without end;
These hard, well-meaning hands we thrust
 Among the heart-strings of a friend.

"The ill-timed truth we might have kept—
 Who knows how sharp it pierced and
  stung!

The word we had not sense to say—
 Who knows how grandly it had
  rung!

"Our faults no tenderness should ask,
   The chastening stripes must cleanse
      them all;
But for our blunders—oh, in shame
   Before the eyes of heaven we fall.

"Earth bears no balsam for mistakes;
   Men crown the knave, and scourge
      the tool
That did his will; but Thou, O Lord,
   Be merciful to me, a fool!"

The room was hushed; in silence rose
   The King, and sought his gardens
      cool,
And walked apart, and murmured low,
   "Be merciful to me, a fool!"

Before Sunrise In Winter

A purple cloud hangs half-way down;
   Sky, yellow gold below;
The naked trees, beyond the town,
   Like masts against it show,—

Bare masts and spars of our earth-ship
   With shining snow-sails furled;
And through the sea of space we slip,
   That flows all around the world.

Eve's Daughter [1887]

I waited in the little sunny room:
  The cool breeze waved the window-lace, at play,
The white rose on the porch was all in bloom,
  And out upon the bay
I watched the wheeling sea-birds go and come.

"Such an old friend,—she would not make me stay
  While she bound up her hair." I turned, and lo,
Danaë in her shower! and fit to slay
  All a man's hoarded prudence at a blow;
Gold hair, that streamed away
  As round some nymph a sunlit fountain's flow.

"She would not make me wait!"—but well I know
  She took a good half-hour to loose and lay
Those locks in dazzling disarrangement so!

Five Lives

Five mites of monads dwelt in a round drop
That twinkled on a leaf by a pool in the sun.
To the naked eye they lived invisible;
Specks, for a world of whom the empty shell
Of a mustard-seed had been a hollow sky.

One was a meditative monad, called a sage;
And, shrinking all his mind within, he thought:
"Tradition, handed down for hours and hours,
Tells that our globe, this quivering crystal world,
Is slowly dying. What if, seconds hence,
When I am very old, yon shimmering dome
Come drawing down and down, till all things end?"
Then with a weazen smirk he proudly felt
No other mote of God had ever gained
Such giant grasp of universal truth.

One was a transcendental monad; thin
And long and slim in the mind; and thus he mused:
"Oh, vast, unfathomable monad-souls
Made in the image"—a hoarse frog croaks from the pool—
"Hark! 't was some god, voicing his glorious thought
In thunder music! Yea, we hear their voice,
And we may guess their minds from ours, their work.
Some taste they have like ours, some tendency
To wriggle about, and munch a trace of scum."
He floated up on a pin-point bubble of gas
That burst, pricked by the air, and he was gone.

One was a barren-minded monad, called
A positivist; and he knew positively:
"There is no world beyond this certain drop.
Prove me another! Let the dreamers dream
Of their faint dreams, and noises from without,
And higher and lower; life is life enough."
Then swaggering half a hair's breadth, hungrily
He seized upon an atom of bug, and fed.

One was a tattered monad, called a poet;
And with shrill voice ecstatic thus he sang:
"Oh, the little female monad's lips!
Oh, the little female monad's eyes:
Ah, the little, little, female, female monad!"

The last was a strong-minded monadess,
Who dashed amid the infusoria,
Danced high and low, and wildly spun and dove
Till the dizzy others held their breath to see.

But while they led their wondrous little lives
Aeonian moments had gone wheeling by,
The burning drop had shrunk with fearful speed;
A glistening film—'t was gone; the leaf was dry.
The little ghost of an inaudible squeak
Was lost to the frog that goggled from his stone;
Who, at the huge, slow tread of a thoughtful ox

Coming to drink, stirred sideways fatly, plunged,
Launched backward twice, and all the pool was still.

Among The Redwoods

Farewell to such a world! Too long I press
    The crowded pavement with unwilling feet.
Pity makes pride, and hate breeds hatefulness,
    And both are poisons. In the forest sweet
The shade, the peace! Immensity, that seems
To drown the human life of doubts and dreams.

Far off the massive portals of the wood,
    Buttressed with shadow, misty-blue, serene,
Waited my coming. Speedily I stood
    Where the dun wall rose roofed in plumy green.
Dare one go in?—Glance backward! Dusk as
        night
Each column, fringed with sprays of amber light.

Let me, along this fallen bole, at rest
    Turn to the cool, dim roof my glowing face.
Delicious dark on weary eyelids prest!
    Enormous solitude of silent space,
But for a low and thunderous ocean sound,
Too far to hear, felt thrilling through the ground.

No stir nor call the sacred hush profanes;
    Save when from some bare tree-top, far on high,
Fierce disputations of the clamorous cranes
    Fall muffled, as from out the upper sky.
So still, one dreads to wake the dreaming air,
Breaks a twig softly, moves the foot with care.

The hollow dome is green with empty shade,
    Struck through with slanted shafts of after-
        noon;

Aloft, a little rift of blue is made,
    Where slips a ghost that last night was the
        moon.
Beside its pearl a sea-cloud stays its wing,
Beneath, a tilted hawk is balancing.

The heart feels not in every time and mood
    What is around it. Dull as any stone
I lay; then, like a darkening dream, the wood
    Grew Karnac's temple, where I breathed alone
In the awed air strange incense, and uprose
Dim, monstrous columns in their dread repose.

The mind not always sees; but if there shine
    A bit of fern-lace bending over moss,
A silky glint that rides a spider-line,
    On a trefoil two shadow spears that cross,
Three grasses that toss up their nodding heads,
With spring and curve like clustered fountain-
        threads,

Suddenly, through side windows of the eye,
    Deep solitudes, where never souls have met;
Vast spaces, forest corridors that lie
    In a mysterious world, unpeopled yet.
Because the outward eye was elsewhere caught,
The awfulness and wonder come unsought.

If death be but resolving back again
    Into the world's deep soul, this is a kind
Of quiet, happy death, untouched by pain
    Or sharp reluctance. For I feel my mind
Is interfused with all I hear and see;
As much a part of All as cloud or tree.

Listen! A deep and solemn wind on high;
    The shafts of shining dust shift to and fro;
The columned trees sway imperceptibly,

And creak as mighty masts when trade-winds
    blow.
The cloudy sails are set; the earth ship swings
Along the sea of space to grander things.

Opportunity [1880]

This I beheld, or dreamed it in a dream:—
There spread a cloud of dust along a plain;
And underneath the cloud, or in it, raged
A furious battle, and men yelled, and swords
Shocked upon swords and shields. A prince's banner
Wavered, then staggered backward, hemmed by foes.
A craven hung along the battle's edge,
And thought, "Had I a sword of keener steel—
That blue blade that the king's son bears,—but this
Blunt thing—!" he snapped and flung it from his hand,
And lowering crept away, and left the field.
Then came the king's son, wounded, sore bestead,
And weaponless, and saw the broken sword,
Hilt-buried in the dry and trodden sand,
And ran and snatched it, and with battle-shout
Lifted afresh he hewed his enemy down,
And saved a great cause that heroic day.

WILL CARLETON [1845-1912]

Will Carleton was raised on his family's farm in Hudson, Michigan. As a child, he exhibited all the traits of a quiet, sensitive and dreamy personality whose avid interest was reading. After finishing his years in school, he found work as a reporter in Chicago. It is known that the appearance of his first poem "Betsy and I Are Out" is linked to a particular instance when he had to write a newspaper article on the issue of divorce. In 1894, he started a monthly journal called *Everywhere* which contained poetry, short stories, and current events. His most famous poem, however, "Over the Hill to the Poorhouse" appeared in the collection entitled *Farm Ballads* (1873) which sold over 40,000 copies. No doubt, because of his intimate familiarity with country life, Carleton is usually acclaimed for his sympathetic, sentimental depiction of farm life among the poor. His major works include *Poems* (1871), *Farm Legends* (1875), *Farm Festivals* (1881), *City Legends* (1889), *City Festivals* (1892), and *Song of Two Centuries* (1902).

Out of The Old House, Nancy

Out of the old house, Nancy—moved up
                into the new;
All the hurry and worry is just as good as
                through.
Only a bounden duty remains for you
                and I —
And that's to stand on the doorstep
                here, and bid the old house good-
                by.

What a shell we've lived in, these nineteen
                or twenty years!
Wonder it hadn't smashed in, and tumbled
                about our ears;
Wonder it's stuck together, and answered
                till to-day;
But every individual log was put up here
                to stay.

Things looked rather new, though, when
                this old house was built;
And things that blossomed you would've
                made some women wilt;
And every other day, then, as sure as day
                would break,
My neighbor Ager come this way, invitin'
                me to "shake."

And you, for want of neighbors, was some-
                times blue and sad,
For wolves and bears and wildcats was the
                nearest ones you had;
But, lookin' ahead to the clearin', we
                worked with all our might,
Until we was fairly out of the woods, and
                things was goin' right.

Look up there at our new house!—ain't it
            a thing to see?
Tall and big and handsome, and new as new
            can be;
All in apple-pie order, especially the
            shelves,
And never a debt to say but what we own
            it all ourselves.

Look at our old log-house—how little it
            now appears!
But it's never gone back on us for nineteen
            or twenty years;
An' I won't go back on it now, or go to
            pokin' fun—
There's such a thing as praisin' a thing for
            the good that it has done.

Probably you remember how rich we was
            that night,
When we was fairly settled, an' had things
            snug and tight:
We feel as proud as you please, Nancy,
            over our house that's new,
But we felt as proud under this old roof,
            and a good deal prouder, too.

Never a handsomer house was seen beneath
            the sun:
Kitchen and parlor and bedroom—we
            had 'em all in one;
And the fat old wooden clock, that we
            bought when we come West,
Was tickin' away in the corner there, and
            doin' its level best.

Trees was all around us, a-whisperin' cheer-
            ing words;
Loud was the squirrel's chatter, and sweet

the songs of birds;
And home grew sweeter and brighter—our
    courage began to mount—
And things looked hearty and happy then,
    and work appeared to count.

And here one night, it happened, when
    things was goin' bad,
We fell in a deep old quarrel—the first
    we ever had;
And when you give out and cried, then I,
    like a fool, give in,
And then we agreed to rub all out, and start
    the thing ag'in.

Here it was, you remember, we sat when
    the day was done,
And you was a-makin' clothing *that wasn't
    for either one;*
And often a soft word of love I was soft
    enough to say,
And the wolves was howlin' in the woods
    not twenty rods away.

The New Church Organ

They've got a bran new organ, Sue,
    For all their fuss and search;
They've done just as they said they'd do,
    And fetched it into church.
They're bound the critter shall be seen,
    And on the preacher's right,
They've hoisted up their new machine
    In everybody's sight.
They've got a chorister and choir,
    Ag'in *my* voice and vote;
For it was never *my* desire

To praise the Lord by note!

I've been a sister good an' true,
    For five an' thirty year;
I've done what seemed my part to do,
    An' prayed my duty clear;
I've sung the hymns both slow and quick,
    Just as the preacher read;
And twice, when Deacon Tubbs was sick,
    I took the fork an' led!
An' now, their bold, new-fangled ways
    Is comin' all about;
And I, right in my latter days,
    Am fairly crowded out!

To-day, the preacher, good old dear,
    With tears all in his eyes,
Read—"I can read my title clear
    To mansions in the skies."—
I al'ays liked that blessed hymn—
    I s'pose I al'ays will;
It somehow gratifies *my* whim,
    In good old Ortonville;
But when that choir got up to sing,
    I couldn't catch a word;
They sung the most dog-gonedest thing
    A body ever heard!

Some worldly chaps was standin' near,
    An' when I see them grin,
I bid farewell to every fear,
    And boldly waded in.
I thought I'd chase the tune along,
    An' tried with all my might;
But though my voice is good an' strong,
    I couldn't steer it right.
When they was high, then I was low,
    An' also contra'wise;
And I too fast, or they too slow,
    To "mansions in the skies."

An' after every verse, you know,
    They played a little tune;
I didn't understand, an' so
    I started in too soon.
I pitched it purty middlin' high,
    And fetched a lusty tone,
But O, alas! I found that I
    Was singin' there alone!
They laughed a little, I am told;
    But I had done my best;

And not a wave of trouble rolled
    Across my peaceful breast.

And Sister Brown,—I could but look,—
    She sits right front of me;
She never was no singin' book,
    An' never went to be;
But then she al'ays tried to do
    The best she could, she said;
She understood the time, right through,
    An' kep' it with her head;
But when she tried this mornin', O,
    I had to laugh, or cough!
It kep' her head a bobbin' so,
    It e'en a'most come off!

An' Deacon Tubbs,—he all broke down,
    As one might well suppose;
He took one look at Sister Brown,
    And meekly scratched his nose.
He looked his hymn-book through and through,
    And laid it on the seat,
And then a pensive sigh he drew,
    And looked completely beat.
An' when they took another bout,
    He didn't even rise;
But drawed his red bandanner out,

An wiped his weepin' eyes.

I've been a sister, good an' true,
    For five an' thirty year;
I've done what seemed my part to do,
    An' prayed my duty clear;
But death will stop my voice, I know,
    For he is on my track;
And some day, I'll to meetin' go,
    And nevermore come back.
And when the folks get up to sing—
    Whene'er that time shall be—

I do not want no *patent* thing
    A squealin' over me!

EMMA LAZARUS [1849-1887]

Emma Lazarus was born into a cultured and well-to-do Jewish family from New York City. Educated at home, she was extremely shy and found refuge in the study of foreign languages and classical literature. Nevertheless, at an early age, she also began to exhibit considerable independence in other areas, and, by the time she was sixteen, she produced her first book of verse which furnished ample proof that she was a gifted poet and writer. Lazarus is perhaps best remembered for a deep interest in Judaic history and an intense devotion to the cause of Jews around the world. This is made evident in her poetry which has been acclaimed by men of superior ideals in Europe as well as America. Her poems are sometimes melancholy, but they are, nonetheless, often patriotic and inspiring. It is not surprising, therefore, that the poem "The New Colossus" is quoted on the base of the Statue of Liberty.

The New Colossus [1883]

Not like the brazen giant of Greek fame,
With conquering limbs astride from land to land;
Here at our sea-washed, sunset gates shall stand
A mighty woman with a torch, whose flame
Is the imprisoned lightning, and her name
Mother of Exiles. From her beacon-hand
Glows world-wide welcome; her mild eyes command
The air-bridged harbor that twin cities frame.
"Keep, ancient lands, your storied pomp!" cries she
With silent lips. "Give me your tired, your poor,
Your huddled masses yearning to breathe free,
The wretched refuse of your teeming shore.
Send these, the homeless, tempest-tost to me,
I lift my lamp beside the golden door!"

Chopin

I.

A dream of interlinking hands, of feet
        Tireless to spin the unseen, fairy woof
Of the entangling waltz. Bright eyebeams meet,
        Gay laughter echoes from the vaulted roof.
Warm perfumes rise; the soft unflickering glow
        Of branching lights sets off the changeful
        charms
Of glancing gems, rich stuffs, the dazzling snow
        Of necks unkerchieft, and bare, clinging arms.
Hark to the music! How beneath the strain
        Of reckless revelry, vibrates and sobs
One fundamental chord of constant pain,
        The pulse-beat of the poet's heart that throbs.
So yearns, though all the dancing waves rejoice,
The troubled sea's disconsolate, deep voice.

II.

Who shall proclaim the golden fable false
    Of Orpheus' miracles? This subtle strain
    Above our prose world's sordid loss and gain
Lightly uplifts us. With the rhythmic waltz,
The lyric prelude, the nocturnal song
    Of love and languor, varied visions rise,
    That melt and blend to our enchanted eyes.
The Polish poet who sleeps silenced long,
    The seraph-souled musician, breathes again
    Eternal eloquence, immortal pain.
Revived the exalted face we know so well,
    The illuminated eyes, the fragile frame,
    Slowly consuming with its inward flame—
We stir not, speak not, lest we break the spell.

III.

A voice was needed, sweet and true and fine
    As the sad spirit of the evening breeze,
Throbbing with human passion, yet divine
    As the wild bird's untutored melodies.
A voice for him 'neath twilight heavens dim,
    Who mourneth for his dead, while round him
    fall
The wan and noiseless leaves. A voice for him
    Who sees the first green sprout, who hears
    the call
Of the first robin on the first spring day.
    A voice for all whom Fate hath set apart,
Who, still misprized, must perish by the way,
    Longing with love, for that they lack the art
Of their own soul's expression. For all these
Sing the unspoken hope, the vague, sad reveries.

IV.

Then Nature shaped a poet's heart,— a lyre
    From out whose chords the slightest breeze
      that blows
Drew trembling music, wakening sweet desire.
    How shall she cherish him? Behold! she
      throws
This precious, fragile treasure in the whirl
    Of seething passions: he is scourged and
      stung;
Must dive in storm-vext seas, if but one pearl
    Of art or beauty therefrom may be wrung.
No pure-browed pensive nymph his Muse shall be:
    An Amazon of thought with sovereign eyes,
    Whose kiss was poison, man-brained, worldly-
      wise,
Inspired that elfin, delicate harmony.
    Rich gain for us! But with him is it well?—
    The poet who must sound earth, heaven, and
      hell!

Mater Amabilis

Down the goldenest of streams,
    Tide of dreams,
The fair cradled man-child drifts;
Sways with cadenced motion slow,
    To and fro,
As the mother-foot poised lightly, falls and
    lifts.

He, the firstling,—he, the light
    Of her sight,—
He, the breathing pledge of love,

'Neath the holy passion lies,
Of her eyes,—
Smiles to feel the warm, life-giving ray above.

She believes that in his vision,
Skies elysian
O'er an angel-people shine.
Back to gardens of delight,
Taking flight,
His auroral spirit basks in dreams divine.

But she smiles through anxious tears;
Unborn years
Pressing forward, she perceives.
Shadowy muffled shapes, they come
Deaf and dumb,
Bringing what? dry chaff and tares, or full-
eared sheaves?

What for him shall she invoke?
Shall the oak
Bind the man's triumphant brow?
Shall his daring foot alight
On the height?
Shall he dwell amidst the humble and the
low?

Through what tears and sweat and pain,
Must he gain
Fruitage from the tree of life?
Shall it yield him bitter flavor?
Shall its savor
Be as manna midst the turmoil and the strife?

In his cradle slept and smiled
Thus the child
Who as Prince of Peace was hailed.
Thus anigh the mother breast,
Lulled to rest,

Child-Napoleon down the lilied river sailed.

Crowned or crucified—the same
    Glows the flame
Of her deathless love divine.
Still the blessed mother stands,
    In all the lands,
As she watched beside thy cradle and by
        mine.

Whatso gifts the years bestow,
    Still men know,
While she breathes, lives one who sees
(Stand they pure or sin-defiled)
    But the child
Whom she crooned to sleep and rocked upon
        her knees.

JAMES WHITCOMB RILEY [1849-1916]

Born in Greenfield, Indiana, James Whitcomb Riley showed an early talent for art, music, and literature. While still a teenager, he contributed poetry to various publications and supported himself by working at a local newspaper. Although this kind of employment seemed to offer him the most secure prospects for the future, at one point, he contrived a public joke, the famous "Leonainie Hoax," in the course of which he managed to have a poem wrongly attributed to Edgar Allan Poe. As a result, he lost his job. Subsequently, he wrote for other papers, especially the *Indianapolis Journal*. Riley, sometimes affectionately known as the "Hoosier Poet," is noted for his treatment of simple, homespun subjects as, for example, in the well-known poem "When Frost Is On The Punkin".

When She Comes Home

When she comes home again! A thou-
    sand ways
I fashion, to myself, the tenderness
Of my glad welcome: I shall tremble—
    yes;
And touch her, as when first in the old days
I touched her girlish hand, nor dared up-
    raise
Mine eyes, such was my faint heart's sweet
    distress.
Then silence: and the perfume of her dress:
The room will sway a little, and a haze
Cloy eyesight—soulsight, even—for a
    space;
And tears—yes; and the ache here in the
    throat,
To know that I so ill deserve the place
Her arms make for me; and the sobbing
    note
I stay with kisses, ere the tearful face
Again is hidden in the old embrace.

The Speeding of the King's Spite

A King—estranged from his loving
          Queen
     By a foolish royal whim—
Tired and sick of the dull routine
     Of matters surrounding him—
Issued a mandate in this wise:—
     "The dower of my daughter's hand
I will give to him who holds this prize,
     The strangest thing in the land."

But the King, sad sooth! in this grim
          decree
     Had a motive low and mean;—
'Twas a royal piece of chicanery
     To harry and spite the Queen;
For King though he was, and beyond
          compare,
     He had ruled all things save one—
Then blamed the Queen that his only
          heir
     Was a daughter—not a son.

The girl had grown, in the mother's
          care,
     Like a bud in the shine and shower
That drinks of the wine of the balmy
          air
     Till it blooms into matchless flowers;
Her waist was the rose's stem that bore
     The flower—and the flower's per-
          fume—
That ripens on till it bulges o'er
     With its wealth of bud and bloom.

And she had a lover—lowly sprung,—
     But a purer, nobler heart

Never spake in a courtlier tongue
    Or wooed with a dearer art:
And the fair pair paled at the King's
        decree;
    But the smiling Fates contrived
To have them wed, in a secrecy
    That the Queen *herself* connived—

While the grim King's heralds scoured
      the land
    And the countries roundabout,
Shouting aloud, at the King's com-
      mand,
    A challenge to knave or lout,
Prince or peasant,—"The mighty King
    Would have ye understand
That he who shows him the strangest
      thing
    Shall have his daughter's hand!"

And thousands flocked to the royal
      throne,
    Bringing a thousand things
Strange and curious;—One, a bone—
    The hinge of a fairy's wings;
And one, the glass of a mermaid queen,
    Gemmed with a diamond dew,
Where, down in its reflex, dimly seen,
    Her face smilèd out at you.

One brought a cluster of some strange
      date,
    With a subtle and searching tang
That seemed, as you tasted, to pene-
      trate
    The heart like a serpent's fang;
And back you fell for a spell entranced,
    As cold as a corpse of stone,
And heard your brains, as they laughed

and danced
And talked in an undertone.
One brought a bird that could whistle
a tune
So piercingly pure and sweet,
That tears would fall from the eyes of
the moon
In dewdrops at its feet,
And the winds would sigh at the sweet
refrain,
Till they swooned in an ecstasy,
To waken again in a hurricane
Of riot and jubilee.

One brought a lute that was wrought
of a shell
Luminous as the shine
Of a new-born star in a dewy dell,—
And its strings were strands of wine
That sprayed at the Fancy's touch and
fused,
As your listening spirit leant
Drunken through with the airs that
oozed
From the o'ersweet instrument.

One brought a tablet of ivory
Whereon no thing was writ,—
But, at night—and the dazzled eyes
would see
Flickering lines o'er it,—
And each, as you read from the magic
tome,
Lightened and died in flame,
And the memory held but a golden
poem
Too beautiful to name.

Till it seemed all the marvels that ever

were known
Or dreamed of under the sun
Were brought and displayed at the
        royal throne,
And put by, one by one;—
Till a graybeard monster came to the
        King—
Haggard and wrinkled and old—
And spread to his gaze this wondrous
        thing,—
A gossamer veil of gold.—

Strangely marvelous—mocking the
        gaze
Like a tangle of bright sunshine,
Dipping a million glittering rays
In a baptism divine:
And a maiden, sheened in this gauze
        attire—
Sifting a glance of her eye—
Dazzled men's souls with a fierce de-
        sire
To kiss and caress her and—die.

And the grim King swore by his royal
        beard
That the veil had won the prize,
While the gray old monster blinked
        and leered
With his lashless, red-rimmed eyes,
As the fainting form of the princess
        fell,
And the mother's heart went wild,
Throbbing and swelling a muffled knell
For the dead hopes of her child.

But her clouded face with a faint
        smile shone,
As suddenly, through the throng,

Pushing his way to the royal throne,
    A fair youth strode along,
While a strange smile hovered about
            his eyes,
        As he said to the grim old King:—
"The veil of gold must lose the prize;
    For *I* have a stranger thing."

He bent and whispered a sentence
            brief;
        But the monarch shook his head,
With a look expressive of unbelief—
    "It can't be so," he said;
"Or give me proof; and I, the King,
    Give you my daughter's hand,—
For certes THAT *is* a stranger thing—
    The strangest thing in the land!"

Then the fair youth, turning, caught
            the Queen
        In a rapturous caress,
While his lithe form towered in lordly
            mien,
        As he said in a brief address:—
"My fair bride's mother is this; and, lo,
    As you stare in your royal awe,
By this pure kiss do I proudly show
    A love for a mother-in-law!"

Then a thaw set in the old King's
            mood,
        And a sweet Spring freshet came
Into his eyes, and his heart renewed
    Its love for the favored dame:
But often he has been heard to declare
    That "he never could clearly see
How, in the deuce, such a strange
            affair
        Could have ended to happily!"

While The Musician Played

O it was but a dream I had
      While the musician played!—
And here the sky, and here the glad
      Old ocean kissed the glade;
And here the laughing ripples ran,
      And here the roses grew
That threw a kiss to every man
      That voyaged with the crew.

Our silken sails in lazy folds
      Drooped in the breathless breeze:
As o'er a field of marigolds
      Our eyes swam o'er the seas;
While here the eddies lisped and purled
      Around the island's rim,
And up from out the underworld
      We saw the mermen swim.

And it was dawn and middle-day
      And midnight—for the moon
On silver rounds across the bay
      Had climbed the skies of June,—
And there the glowing, glorious king
      Of day ruled o'er his realm,
With stars of midnight glittering
      About his diadem.

The sea-gull reeled on languid wing
      In circles round the mast,
We heard the songs the sirens sing
      As we went sailing past;
And up and down the golden sands
      A thousand fairy throngs
Flung at us from their flashing hands
      The echoes of their songs.

O it was but a dream I had

While the musician played!—
For here the sky, and here the glad
Old ocean kissed the glade;

And here the laughing ripples ran,
And here the roses grew
That threw a kiss to every man
That voyaged with the crew.

Elizabeth

MAY 1, 1891

I

Elizabeth! Elizabeth!
The first May-morning whispereth
Thy gentle name in every breeze
That lispeth through the young-leaved
          trees,
New raimented in white and green
Of bloom and leaf to crown the
          queen;—
And, as in odorous chorus, all
The orchard-blossoms sweetly call
Even as a singing voice that saith,
          Elizabeth! Elizabeth!

II

Elizabeth! Lo, lily-fair,
In deep, cool shadows of thy hair,
Thy face maintaineth its repose—
Is it, O sister of the rose,
So better, sweeter, blooming thus

Than in this bricry world with us?
    Where frost o'ertaketh, and the
        breath
Of biting winter harrieth
With sleeted rains and blighting snow
    All fairest blooms—Elizabeth!

III

Nay, then!—So reign, Elizabeth,
Crowned, in thy May-day realm of
        death!
Put forth the scepter of thy love
In every star-tipped blossom of
The grassy dais of thy throne!
Sadder are we, thus left alone,
But gladder they that thrill to see
Thy mother's rapture, greeting thee
    Bereaved are we by life—not death—
        Elizabeth! Elizabeth!

The Old Swimmin'-Hole

Oh! the old swimmin'-hole! whare
        the crick so still and deep
Looked like a baby-river that was lay-
        ing half asleep,
And the gurgle of the worter round
        the drift jest below
Sounded like the laugh of something
        we onc't ust to know
Before we could remember anything
        but the eyes
Of the angels lookin' out as we left
        Paradise;
But the merry days of youth is beyond
        our controle,

And it's hard to part ferever with the
    old swimmin'-hole.

Oh! the old swimmin'-hole! In the
    happy days of yore,
When I ust to lean above it on the
    old sickamore,
Oh! it showed me a face in its warm
    sunny tide
That gazed back at me so gay and
    glorified,
It made me love myself, as I leaped to
    caress
My shadder smilin' up at me with sich
    tenderness.
But them days is past and gone, and
    old Time's tuck his toll
From the old man come back to the
    old swimmin'-hole.

Oh! the old swimmin'-hole! In the
    long, lazy days
When the humdrum of school made
    so many run-a-ways,
How plesant was the jurney down the
    old dusty lane,
Whare the tracks of our bare feet was
    all printed so plane
You could tell by the dent of the heel
    and the sole
They was lots o' fun on hands at the
    old swimmin'-hole.
But the lost joys is past! Let your
    tears in sorrow roll
Like the rain that ust to dapple up the
    old swimmin'-hole.

Thare the bullrushes growed, and the
    cattails so tall,

And the sunshine and shadder fell over
    it all;

And it mottled the worter with amber
    and gold
Tel the glad lilies rocked in the ripples
    that rolled;
And the snake-feeder's four gauzy
    wings fluttered by
Like the ghost of a daisy dropped out
    of the sky,
Or a wownded apple-blossom in the
    breeze's controle
As it cut acrost some orchurd to'rds the
    old swimmin'-hole.

Oh! the old swimmin'-hole! When I
    last saw the place,
The scenes was all changed, like the
    change in my face;
The bridge of the railroad now crosses
    the spot
Whare the old divin'-log lays sunk and
    fergot.
And I stray down the banks whare the
    trees ust to be—
But never again will theyr shade
    shelter me!
And I wish in my sorrow I could strip
    to the soul,
And dive off in my grave like the old
    swimmin'-hole.

Green Fields and Running Brooks

Ho! green fields and running
            brooks!
Knotted strings and fishing-hooks

Of the truant, stealing down
Weedy back-ways of the town.

Where the sunshine overlooks,
By green fields and running brooks,
All intruding guests of chance
With a golden tolerance.

Cooing doves, or pensive pair
Of picnickers, straying there—
By green fields and running brooks,
Sylvan shades and mossy nooks!

And—O Dreamer of the Days,
Murmurer of roundelays
All unsung of words or books,
Sing green fields and running brooks.

When the Frost is on the Punkin

When the frost is on the punkin and the fodder's
    in the shock,
And you hear the kyouck and gobble of the strut-
    tin' turkey-cock,
And the clackin' of the guineys, and the cluckin'
    of the hens,
And the rooster's hallylooyer as he tiptoes on the
    fence;

O it's then's the times a feller is a-feelin' at his
    best.
With the risin' sun to greet him from a night of
    peaceful rest,
As he leaves the house, bare-headed, and goes out
    to feed the stock,
When the frost is on the punkin and the fodder's
    in the shock.

They's something kindo' harty-like about the at-
    musfere
When the heat of summer's over and the coolin'
    fall is here—
Of course we miss the flowers, and the blossums on
    the trees,
And the mumble of the hummin'-birds and buzzin'
    of the bees;
But the air's so appetizin'; and the landscape
    through the haze
Of a crisp and sunny morning of the airly autumn
    days
Is a pictur' that no painter has the colorin' to
    mock—
When the frost is on the punkin and the fodder's
    in the shock.

The husky, rusty russel of the tossels of the corn,

And the raspin' of the tangled leaves, as golden
     as the morn;
The stubble in the furries—kindo' lonesome-like,
     but still
A-preachin' sermuns to us of the barns they
     growed to fill;
The strawstack in the medder, and the reaper in
     the shed;
The hosses in theyr stalls below—the clover over-
     head!—
O, it sets my hart a-clickin' like the tickin' of a
     clock,
When the frost is on the punkin and the fodder's
     in the shock.

ERNEST FRANCISCO FENOLLOSA [1853-1908]

Ernest Francisco Fenollosa was born in Salem, Massachusetts. While his mother was of Colonial ancestry, his father was a musician of Spanish descent. Upon graduating from Harvard in 1874, he went to the University of Tokyo where he taught politics, economics, philosophy, logic and developed a lasting personal interest in Japanese art. This experience, in turn, proved useful back home. Upon returning to the United States in 1890, he became curator of Oriental art at the Boston Musuem and wrote poetry which reflected his fascination with the East. His scholarly endeavors also served as an inspiration for Ezra Pound's *Cathay* (1915). Among his major works are *Poetry—East and West* and *The Discovery of America and Other Poems* (1893).

The Golden Age

This world was not
    As it now is seen:
It once was clothed
    With a deeper green;
And rarer gems
    Than the ice-caves hold
The sea brought up
    On the sands of gold.

But rust of ages,
    The breath of Time,
The meadows covered
    With early rime;
And the wild grass faded,
    The gems were gone,
And the wave fell cold
    As it thundered on.

In bygone ages
    The world was fair,
And the moon-god played
    With her golden hair;
And the paling stars
    With love-white arms
Bent down to welcome
    A sister's charms.

The air lay sweet
    With the breath of pines;
The hill-tops glowed
    With their wealth of mines;
And sweet, and low,
    And rich, and free,
The wild, dark music
    Stole over the sea.

And the sea-waves laughed
    At the saffron moon;
And the musk-rose smiled
    With her soul of June;
And the golden age
    Of Nature's years
No warning heard
    Of her coming tears.

But the hand of man
    Was the sword of death:
A poison lurked
    In his savage breath,
And the wealth of years
    And the glow of years
Were drowned in a flood
    Of swelling tears.

The world was fair
    In the days of yore;
But that golden age
    Shall come no more.
The sun may shine,
    And wild flowers bloom;
But the goal of all
    Is the open tomb,—

The end of all
    Is the silent grave;
And beauty lies
    In the cold still wave.
And the world shall harden
    The hearts of men
Till it hear the voice
    Of its Christ again.

HENRY CUYLER BUNNER [1855-1896]

Henry Cuyler Bunner was born in Oswego, New York, raised in New York City, and spent most of his married life in Nutley, Nw Jersey. In spite of frail health, he led an active life and was known among friends as a man of great wit and phenomenal memory. As a writer, he wrote short stories, plays, and especially poetry which is striking for its light, lyrical quality. Bunner never attended college and made a living as an editor. His major works include *Airs from Arcady and Elsewhere* (1884), *Rowan/ Second Crop Songs* (1892), *The Poems of H. C. Bunner* (1896), *Three Operettas* (1897).

The Way To Arcady

Oh, what's the way to Arcady,
    To Arcady, to Arcady;
Oh, what's the way to Arcady,
    Where all the leaves are merry?

Oh, what's the way to Arcady?
The spring is rustling in the tree,—
The tree the wind is blowing through,—
    It sets the blossoms flickering white.
I knew not skies could burn so blue
    Nor any breezes blow so light.
They blow an old-time way for me,
Across the world to Arcady.

Oh, what's the way to Arcady?
Sir Poet, with the rusty coat,
Quit mocking of the song-bird's note.
How have you heart for any tune,
You with the wayworn russet shoon?

Your scrip, a-swinging by your side,
Gapes with a gaunt mouth hungry-wide.
I'll brim it well with pieces red,
If you will tell the way to tread.

Oh, I am bound for Arcady,
And if you but keep pace with me
You tread the way to Arcady.

And where away lies Arcady,
And how long yet may the journey be?

Ah, that (quoth he) *I do not know:*
Across the clover and the snow—
Across the frost, across the flowers—
Through summer seconds and winter hours
I've trod the way my whole life long,

And know not now where it may be;
My guide is but the stir to song,
That tells me I cannot go wrong,
    Or clear or dark the pathway be
    Upon the road to Arcady.

But how shall I do who cannot sing?
    I was wont to sing, once on a time,—
There is never an echo now to ring
    Remembrance back to the trick of rhyme.

'Tis strange you cannot sing (quoth he),—
The folk all sing in Arcady.

But how may he find Arcady
Who hath nor youth nor melody?

What, know you not, old man (quoth he),—
    Your hair is white, your face is wise,—
    That Love must kiss that Mortal's eyes
Who hopes to see fair Arcady?
No gold can buy you entrance there;
But beggared Love may go all bare—
No wisdom won with weariness;
But Love goes in with Folly's dress—
No fame that wit could ever win;
But only Love may lead Love in
    To Arcady, to Arcady.

Ah, woe is me, through all my days
    Wisdom and wealth I both have got,
And fame and name, and great men's
            praise;
    But Love, ah Love! I have it not.
There was a time, when life was new—
    But far away, and half forgot—
I only know her eyes were blue;
    But Love—I fear I knew it not.
We did not wed, for lack of gold,

And she is dead, and I am old.
All things have come since then to me,
Save Love, ah Love ! and Arcady.

Ah, then I fear we part (quoth he),—
My way's for Love and Arcady.

But you, you fare alone, like me;
    The gray is likewise in your hair.
What love have you to lead you there,
To Arcady, to Arcady?

Ah, no, not lonely do I fare;
    My true companion's Memory.
With Love he fills the Spring-time air;
    With Love he clothes the Winter tree.
Oh, past this poor horizon's bound
    My song goes straight to one who stands,—
Her face all gladdening at the sound,—
    To lead me to the Spring-green lands,
To wander with enlacing hands.

The songs within my breast that stir
Are all of her, are all of her.
My maid is dead long years (quoth he),—
She waits for me in Arcady.

Oh, yon's the way to Arcady,
    To Arcady, to Arcady;
Oh, yon's the way to Arcady,
    Where all the leaves are merry.

She Was A Beauty

She was a beauty in the days
    When Madison was President,
And quite coquettish in her ways,—
    On conquests of the heart intent.

    Grandpapa, on his right knee bent,
Wooed her in stiff, old-fashioned phrase,—
She was a beauty in the days
    When Madison was President.

    And when your roses where hers went
Shall go, my Rose, who date from Hayes,
    I hope you'll wear her sweet content
Of whom tradition lightly says:
She was a beauty in the days
    When Madison was President.

A Pitcher of Mignonette

A pitcher of mignonette
    In a tenement's highest casement,—
Queer sort of flower-pot—yet
That pitcher of mignonette
Is a garden in heaven set,
    To the little sick child in the basement—
The pitcher of mignonette,
    In the tenement's highest casement.

Shake, Mulleary and Go-ethe

I have a bookcase, which is what
Many much better men have not.
There are no books inside, for books,
I am afraid, might spoil its looks.

But I've three busts, all second-hand,
Upon the top. You understand
I could not put them underneath—
Shake, Mulleary and Go-ethe.

Shake was a dramatist of note;
He lived by writing things to quote.
He long ago put on his shroud;
Some of his works are rather loud.
His baldy spot's dusty, I suppose.
I know there's dust upon his nose.
I'll have to give each nose a sheath—
Shake, Mulleary and Go-ethe.

Mulleary's line was quite the same;
He has more hair, but far less fame.
I would not from that fame retrench—
But he is foreign, being French.
Yet high his haughty head he heaves,
The only one done up in leaves,
They're rather limited on wreath—
Shake, Mulleary and Go-ethe.

Go-ethe wrote in the German tongue:
He must have learned it very young.
His nose is quite a butt for scoff,
Although an inch of it is off.
He did quite nicely for the Dutch;
But here he doesn't count for much.
They all are off their native heath—
Shake, Mulleary and Go-ethe.

They sit there, on their chests, as bland
As if they were not second-hand.
I do not know of what they think,
Nor why they never frown or wink.
But why from smiling they refrain
I think I clearly can explain:

They none of them could show much teeth—
Shake, Mulleary and Go-ethe.

SAM WALTER FOSS [1858-1911]

Sam Walter Foss was born in New Hampshire and graduated from Brown University. Most of his life, he worked as a librarian and pursued personal interests in literature. As a poet, he became known for his esthetic convictions involving a peculiar form of optimistic populism. This did not always meet with approval, especially among critics who felt that poetry should treat elevated—rather than ordinary or simple—subjects. Nevertheless, Foss is generally recognized for his ability to incorporate elements of folk culture and dialect into traditional forms of rhymed, inspirational verse. Perhaps his most famous poem is "The House by the Side of the Road."

The House by the Side of the Road [1898]

*"He was a friend to man, and lived in a house
by the side of the road."*—HOMER

There are hermit souls that live withdrawn
   In the peace of their self-content;
There are souls, like stars, that dwell apart,
   In a fellowless firmament;
There are pioneer souls that blaze their paths
   Where highways never ran;—
But let me live by the side of the road
   And be a friend to man.

Let me live in a house by the side of the road,
   Where the race of men go by—
The men who are good and the men who are bad,
   As good and as bad as I.
I would not sit in the scorner's seat,
   Or hurl the cynic's ban;—
Let me live in a house by the side of the road
   And be a friend to man.

I see from my house by the side of the road,
   By the side of the highway of life,
The men who press with the ardor of hope,
   The men who are faint with the strife.

But I turn not away from their smiles nor their tears—
   Both parts of an infinite plan;—
Let me live in my house by the side of the road
   And be a friend to man.

I know there are brook-gladdened meadows ahead
   And mountains of wearisome height;
That the road passes on through the long afternoon
   And stretches away to the night.
But still I rejoice when the travellers rejoice,
   And weep with the strangers that moan,

Nor live in my house by the side of the road
Like a man who dwells alone.

Let me live in my house by the side of the road
    Where the race of men go by—
They are good, they are bad, they are weak, they are strong,
    Wise, foolish—so am I.
Then why should I sit in the scorner's seat
    Or hurl the cynic's ban?—
Let me live in my house by the side of the road
    And be a friend to man.

The Creedless Man

A creedless love, that knows no clan,
　No caste, no cult, no church but Man;
That deems to-day and now and here,
　Are voice and vision of the seer;
That through this lifted human clod
　The inflow of the breath of God
Still sheds its apostolic powers,—
　Such love, such trust, such faith be ours.

We deem man climbs an endless slope
　Tow'rd far-seen tablelands of hope;
That he, through filth and shame of sin,
　Still seeks the God that speaks within;
That all the years since time began
　Work the eternal Rise of Man;
And all the days that time shall see
　Tend tow'rd the Eden yet to be.

Too long our music-hungering needs
　Have heard the iron clash of creeds.
The creedless love that knows no clan,
　No caste, no cult, no church but Man,
Shall drown with mellow music all,
　The dying jangle of their brawl;—
Some love with all its quickening powers,
　Such love to God and Man be ours.

FRANK DEMPSTER SHERMAN [1860-1916]

Frank Dempster Sherman was born into a distinguished family from Peekskill, New York. He studied architecture at Columbia University and joined the faculty in 1887. Because of his many talents and charming personality, he was highly regarded by his contemporaries. Sherman never achieved the status of a major poet, but he is remembered today for the delightful warmth and humor of his verse. His most famous works are *Madrigals and Catches* (1887), *Lyrics For a Lute* (1890), *Little Folk Lyrics* (1892), and *Lyrics of Joy* (1904).

Her Guitar

By the fire that loves to tint her
　Cheeks the color of a rose,
While the wanton winds of winter
　Lose the landscape in the snows,—
While the air grows keen and bitter,
　And the clean-cut silver stars
Tremble in the cold and glitter
　Through the twilight's dusky bars,—
In a cosey room where lingers
　Happy Time on folded wings,
I am watching five white fingers
　Float across six slender strings
Of an old guitar, held lightly,—
　Captivated while she sets,
Here and there, five others tightly
　　　On the frets.

Lost in loving contemplation
　Of the fair, shy girlish face
Conscious of no admiration,
　Posed with such a charming grace
O'er this instrument some Spanish
　Serenader used to keep
Hidden till the sun would vanish
　And the birds were fast asleep;
Who, below his loved one's casement,
　With the mellow Southern moon
Through a leafy interlacement
　Shining softly, thrummed a tune:
Did she answer it, I wonder?
　Did she frame a sweet reply?
Did she grant the wish made under
　　　Such a sky?

This I know, if she had listened
　To the melody I've heard,
Mute confessions must have glistened

In her eyes at every word;
And the very stars above her
    Must have whispered, one by one,
Something sentimental of her
    When the serenade was done.
For this music has but ended,
    And I leave my dreams to find
With the notes are somehow blended
    Like confessions of my mind;
And the gentle girl who guesses
    What these broken secrets are,
Is the one whose arm caresses
                This guitar.

Daisies

At evening when I go to bed
I see the stars shine overhead;
They are the little daisies white
That dot the meadow of the night.

And often while I'm dreaming so,
Across the sky the moon will go;
It is a lady, sweet and fair,
Who comes to gather daisies there.

For, when at morning I arise,
There's not a star left in the skies;
She's picked them all and dropped them down
Into the meadows of the town.

On A Greek Vase

Divinely shapen cup, thy lip
    Unto me seemeth thus to speak:
"Behold in me the workmanship,
    The grace and cunning of a Greek!

"Long ages since he mixed the clay,
    Whose sense of symmetry was such,
The labor of a single day
    Immortal grew beneath his touch.

"For dreaming while his fingers went
    Around this slender neck of mine,
The form of her he loved was blent
    With every matchless curve and line.

"Her loveliness to me he gave
    Who gave unto herself his heart,
That love and beauty from the grave
    Might rise and live again in art."

And hearing from thy lips this tale
    Of love and skill, of art and grace,
Thou seem'st to me no more the frail
    Memento of an older race:

But in thy form divinely wrought
    And figured o'er with fret and scroll,
I dream, by happy chance was caught,
And dwelleth now, that maiden's soul.

INDEX

Poet names are in bold face; poem titles are in italics; and poem first lines are enclosed in quotation marks.